Bear Market Investing Strategies

WILEY TRADING SERIES

BEAR MARKET INVESTING STRATEGIES

Harry D. Schultz

JOHN WILEY & SONS LTD

Other Wiley Editorial Offices

John Wiley & Sons, Inc., 605 Third Avenue,
New York, NY 10158-0012, USA

Wiley-VCH GmbH, Pappelallee 3,
D-69469 Weinheim, Germany

John Wiley & Sons Australia Ltd, 33 Park Road, Milton,
Queensland 4064, Australia

John Wiley & Sons (Asia) Pte Ltd, 2 Clementi Loop #02-01,
Jin Xing Distripark, Singapore 129809

John Wiley & Sons (Canada) Ltd, 22 Worcester Road,
Rexdale, Ontario M9W 1L1, Canada

Library of Congress Cataloging-in-Publication Data
A Library of Congress record has been applied for

British Library Cataloguing in Publication Data
A catalogue record for this book is available from the British Library

ISBN 0-470-84702-6

Project management by Originator, Gt Yarmouth (typeset in 10/12pt Times)
Printed and bound in Great Britain by TJ International Ltd, Padstow, Cornwall
This book is printed on acid-free paper responsibly manufactured from sustainable forestry,
in which at least two trees are planted for each one used for paper production.

Contents

1
Introduction

"History never looks like history when you are living through it. It always looks confusing and messy, and it always feels uncomfortable."

John W. Gardner, 1968

Over the last 20 years, investors have increasingly come to regard investing in stocks about the same as putting money in the bank—except they got a higher return. This belief became so pervasive that, as recently as 2000, the government in Washington was still talking about putting part of the Social Security account into securities in order to earn a higher return. After the Nasdaq crash, that plan was quietly dropped. Even investors who researched stocks before buying them either mostly used computer programs that rely on past action repeating more or less exactly in order to predict future buy or sell points, or they used Internet advice which in many cases was nothing more than thinly disguised sales pitches.

There is an old adage which says that *knowledge* can be communicated but *wisdom* has to be self-taught. I hope that, by the end of this book, you will have enough knowledge to evolve your own market wisdom.

With the coming of the Internet, investors were so focused on acquiring the latest information on securities that many never bothered to learn how that information could be best used.

And just as many of us have lost the ability to spell correctly or do simple arithmetic because we rely on spell checks and computer calculators, so investors who rely only on the Internet for investment know-how have never had to learn the basic signals to judge where markets will go next. Even more dangerous is the assumption that prediction is a scientific process, whereby if you have the right piece of software that correctly predicted market turning points in the recent past, it would certainly be able to predict the future.

But market analysis is not a science; it is an art, using intuition and experience to make sense of evolving data. Past patterns may at times not have their usual relevance for future predictions.

I have been writing an investment newsletter for 38 years, and I seem to be on virtually every investment mailing list there is.

During the last 5 years of the 1990s, I was inundated with junk mail from software companies claiming to have the key to future market success, based only on their program having called turning points for a few prior years. These software packages used such phrases as: "fully automated trading software," and "built-in portfolio," implying that all you needed to make money in the stock market was knowledge of how to operate their software.

Until the mid-1990s, analysts on financial news programs did useful research and offered informed opinions of where markets in general and specific stocks were likely to go. But increasingly over the subsequent years those same analysts concentrated ever more on being entertainers, as all business news programs became little more than infomercials for their advertisers. The focus became less to seriously inform and more on keeping the viewer watching so the advertisers would have an audience.

But then markets topped out, Nasdaq crashed, and the war on terrorism gave the media permission to use the word "recession," without being accused of "talking down the market." Investors were left wondering what to do with stocks that in many cases had already lost a substantial portion of their value in the prior 2 years. Their "magic bullet" software programs failed them, and they lacked basic market know-how, or how to invest in what appears to be the early stages of a protracted bear market.

This book is designed to upgrade investors' knowledge with the basics of how to make investment decisions, with particular reference to bear markets, bull market corrections and recessions. But simply knowing how to make respectable buy and sell decisions is not enough.

Nobody in the history of Wall Street has ever guessed right all the time. It's therefore necessary not only to decide how to predict market direction, but what strategies to use to minimize losses when you guess wrong, and maximize your profits when you are right.

The ultimate decision for your investments is made by you. Over the nearly 4 decades I have been advising clients, there have been many times when I would give the same advice to three people, and one would make money, one would break even, and one would lose money.

However good the advice we receive, we always inject our own judgment into the equation. In this book, we will discuss how best to make your own informed decisions.

A key principle of technical analysis is that there are certain recurring patterns of investing behavior that can be charted. But no technical tool works all the time. Though history does seem to repeat itself in a general sense, it never repeats exactly, so no one model of past action, be it a war, inflation, civil unrest, or a bear market, is sufficient to ascertain what the future will bring.

After the September 11, 2001 attack on New York and the Pentagon, advisors rushed to predict future markets, based on what the Dow Jones Averages did in the Gulf War, or the Vietnam War. But the war on terrorism is unlike any war in the past. The recession of 2000 seems likely to have variations from a number of past recessions.

The best way to use the past for future projections is to have as much history as possible of past events: market averages, individual stock groups, technical indicators such as Confidence Index or advance/decline lines, wars, government monetary intervention, etc. Then check for similarities to what is happening today. With this data, we can then build a mental big picture for possible future market direction based on elements of as much history as possible, which taken together form a totally new paradigm.

This book discusses past models based on technical analysis and chart reading, plus similar economic, political, war, and social conditions.

Hopefully, by the end of this book, you will have enough information to construct your own market vision for the next several years.

A WARNING

Any composite model view of possible future action is never static. As events change and unfold, your predictive model should be modified. This book is written at a specific point in time. Even if the visions I offer in the later chapters are correct in a general sense, I cannot possibly be correct about the details. It is up to you to update and fine-tune your model as things evolve.

WHAT YOU WILL LEARN

This book offers both the novice and the seasoned investor perspectives on investment theory and strategies, with particular reference to recessionary times.

Chapter 2 defines exactly what a bear market is and how it is different from corrective reactions in a bull market. Wars, terrorism, politics, and social events in the main only affect markets indirectly. What ultimately moves stocks and therefore markets is the underlying value of the companies that those stocks represent. Only inasmuch as those non-market factors affect the underlying economics are they relevant. But the mass media would have you believe otherwise, because with daily air time to fill they report daily trivia.

Economic trends are slow to build and slow to change directions, as are major bull or bear markets, which doesn't make sexy TV talky talk.

Chapter 3 describes past bear markets, as measured by the Dow Jones Industrial Average. The purpose is to create models of what past bear markets looked like, to be used as context when you construct your own view of possible future action.

Chapter 4 lists economic and other general signs that suggest a bull market is ending and a bear market is beginning.

Chapter 5 discusses foreign investment and whether one should put money abroad in a bear market.

Chapter 6 discusses the difference between a bear market rally (secondary reaction) and the beginning of a new bull market.

Chapter 7 is the mirror image of Chapter 6. It discusses down-legs in a bear market and how they differ from reactions in a bull market.

Chapter 8 lists specific technical indicators that you can use for measuring both bull and bear markets (tools which act consistently in both bull and bear markets).

Chapter 9 lists those technical indicators that behave very differently in bear markets to bull markets, so you need to decide which is occurring before you use these indicators.

Chapter 10 discusses the usefulness of Cycles study. Cycles have their modest place in your toolbox of past models of markets, but the past never repeats exactly—as many cycles aficionados would have you believe.

Chapter 11 teaches you about chart reading and chart interpretation. For most people, data in the form of a chart is more meaningful. "A picture speaks a thousand words."

Chapter 12 gives basic rules of investment in a bear market, when preserving capital is more important than risk taking.

Chapter 13 teaches you all you ever wanted to know about short selling.

Chapter 14 is perhaps the most important chapter in the book. No matter how savvy an investor you are, there will be times when you will be quite wrong about the direction of the market. This chapter gives you strategies to enable you to make money, even if you are wrong about market direction sometimes.

Chapter 15 shows no matter whether you are a short-, medium- or long-term trader or investor, you really must develop a more flexible approach to buying and selling in a bear market than in boom times. Bear markets are a lot more volatile than bull markets, so they have to be watched more closely.

Chapter 16 offers you some defensive investments that enable you to sleep nights, some of which you can hold long term. The trick is deciding what *sort* of bear market we are in, before you decide which defensive investments to choose.

Chapters 17 and 18 discuss how human emotions, particularly *your* emotions affect your investment decisions.

By the time you reach Chapter 19, if I have done my job well, you should already have a strong sense of where we might be headed, economically, in securities markets and on a social and governmental level over the next few years.

Chapters 19 and 20 offer my personal overview of the next few years, to give you another context for your decision making.

BE NOT AN OPTIMIST, NOR A PESSIMIST, BUT A REALIST

The hardest part of developing a portfolio in a bear market is human nature's natural optimism. There is a saying that man can live 30 days without food, 7 days without water, but only a few hours without hope. However much your intellect might believe that economic and technical factors point to a protracted bear market, your heart will inject the hope that the data is wrong. The hardest part of making money in a bear market is facing the fact that we are in one, and that, at least for a while, there will be few concrete signals that a critical turnaround is in sight.

But, by the time you reach Chapter 20, you will know enough about bear markets to also know approximately how they end.

BUY WHEN THE BLOOD IS RUNNING IN THE STREETS

On July 8, 1932, the Dow hit a record low of 41, down 90% from its all-time high. It felt as if the disaster would never end. Yet, just a few weeks later, a new bull market began that, for those who bought, saw their investment more than quadruple over the next 5 years.

In 1942, 4 months after the Japanese bombed Pearl Harbor, the Dow crashed to 92. The war loomed large into the future, and buying stocks was the last thing on most people's minds. Yet those "realistic optimists" who bought, in the Spring of 1942, experienced a steady climb in values until the Dow hit 212 in 1946.

In a sense, a bear is more of an optimist than a permanent bull. A permanent bull wants the past to continue forever, and, when it doesn't, he becomes disoriented and/or depressed. But bulls who become bears when markets turn are bigger optimists because they know the downturn will not be permanent and after current problems a better future awaits, one where you can enjoy the fruits of your realistic investment strategies. They never forget that, in spite of setbacks, the history of human societies shows that the super long-term trend is up, and that even a huge bear market is only a multi-year setback in the grand scheme of things.

If you can remind yourself daily that "this too will pass," when most investors are still fearful of buying securities and economic data continue to be negative, but your composite picture of future market action indicates it is time to begin cautiously buying, then you will be buying at the beginning of the next great bull market.

Part I
THE BEAR BACKGROUND

"The whole idea that something is an Internet company *is no more reason to invest in that company than investing in any one of the 508 automobile companies in business around 1910. Only a few of them will be there when the whole thing settles out."*

James Collins, quoted in *The Internet Bubble*, by
Anthony B. Perkins and Michael C. Perkins, Harper Collins, 1999
(the 500 auto makers were reduced to 3)

2
Overview

"Every man takes the limits of his own field of vision for the limits of the world."

Arthur Schopenhauer, 1851

In the late 1950s, when I first started serious stock market investment/analysis, it was only necessary to put your assets into blue chips and watch them appreciate year after year. But, by the late 1960s and throughout the 1970s, the key to making money in markets was not just buying sound companies, but understanding Vietnam War-induced inflation, as government tried to supply both "guns and butter." (Just as the US is doing today.)

By the early 1970s, it was also necessary to have some understanding of foreign markets and international affairs, when OPEC, seeing their pound and dollar assets already eroding because of fiscal irresponsibility in both the US and Britain, temporarily cut off the West's oil supply using the 1967 Arab–Israeli Six Day War as the excuse.

And, as the value of the dollar declined, the value of the Swiss franc and the German mark rose sharply, so it was possible to make a great deal of money simply by moving out of US dollars and into Euro currencies and bonds.

THE BEAR AND HIS MARKET

Since this book is largely about bear markets, it seems necessary to give a dependable *definition* of both a bear and bear markets.

A bear is an investor or trader who believes the trend of stock prices is down and trades or invests with that trend by selling his stock and/or selling short.

A bear market is a depressed or declining market. One can have a bear market in real estate, advertising, automobiles, art, commodities, bonds, or anything else—including the stock market.

A bear market in stocks is usually defined in ways that equate the mini-bear markets of 1983, 1987, and 1990 with the more prolonged bear markets we saw in the 1970s or even with the great bear market that began in 1929. I prefer to define bear markets in three categories:

1.   Baby bears such as those we have seen during the last 20 years, which were little more than secondary reactions within a papa bull trend.
2.   Mama bear markets such as we saw in 1973–74.
3.   Papa bear markets such as the one from 1929 to 1942 and, in constant dollar terms, from 1966 to 1981. (See *Constant Dollar Dow* chart in Chapter 19.) Within these major bear markets, it is possible to have mini and medium size bull markets (more on this in the next chapter), but what makes them still a bear market, in spite of huge up-moves, is that the original damage to market and economic infrastructure is *not solved* until the end of the cycle. For example, it was not until the mini-bear of 1981 that the problem of inflation was solved, enabling the stock market and business to begin a major new bull market.

During the last 20 years, many analysts have forgotten that, although when you buy or sell a stock you are at that moment simply making a bet with another investor on the future direction of that stock, you are not just buying a lottery ticket. You are buying a piece of a company. Therefore, it matters over the medium and longer term whether that company will succeed or fail. Today, it seems fashionable to divorce the *value* of a stock from its price. That was almost valid during the late great bubble, but may not be so again in our lifetime. New bubbles arise only when the last one is forgotten, usually in a new generation.

BE NOT A BULL, NOR A BEAR, BUT A REALIST

A bear is not (at least should not be) a permanent pessimist. Nor should a bull always be an optimist if he is wise. Both should try hard to be realists. You should be able to change from a bull to a bear or a bear to a bull, as conditions change, and not be the least inconsistent. Some people *are* permanent bears, and give the symbol a bad name. Permanent bears often have a puritan ideology that sees prosperity and bullishness as some kind of Original Sin.

Likewise, many people are always bullish, obviously without sufficient justification. The almost continual bull market from 1982 to March 2000 has made most people permanent bulls. It has been impossible for them to accept that any downturn is more than a short-term correction. But, in any market, the flexible realist is the winner—the man or woman who can switch directions overnight.

So, let it be crystal clear that a proper bear is someone who used to be a bull but became a bear as conditions changed.

SHORT SELLING—IT'S NOT UNPATRIOTIC

Before going further, let me give a definition of short selling because it's vital to what follows, and I don't take up the subject in detail until much later. Short selling is the opposite of normal (long) stock positions. If you buy a stock hoping it will go up, you are "long" of the stock. But if you think the stock will go down, you can sell it first, and buy it anytime you please. This "short selling" is a simple borrowing-of-stock process that is handled by your broker with no need for you to understand how.

Now, let me clear the air on another common fallacy that some people hold with regard to bears. Some think being a bear and/or selling short is in some way unpatriotic or negative. They believe that to invest your money in the industry of your country and lose it is more patriotic than to "sell those industries short" by selling their stock short—or simply selling out completely because you feel we have entered a bear market.

Many TV market commentators, in the aftermath of the September 11, 2001 terrorist attack, urged investors to hold on to their stocks regardless of what the markets would do. At the beginning of G.W. Bush's presidency, when he suggested that there were signs of weakness in the US economy, there was a cry of outrage from those who accused him of *talking down* the stock market and the economy—as if the health of our entire capitalist system is so fragile that it can be *talked* into changing directions.

Even advisors claiming to help you recession-proof your portfolio cite people like Warren Buffet who made his fortune by buying and holding, regardless of short- and medium-term fluctuations. Most advise all non-professional investors to do the same, unless they are getting near retirement age, when switching into "bonds might be safer." What these advisors fail to mention is that it is only since 1982 that buying and holding has paid off over the longer term. But Joseph Kennedy, father of JFK, for example, made his family's fortune by short selling in the bear market that began in 1929. And many lesser known tycoons of the roaring twenties simply sold all their stocks and took a multi-year vacation, beginning around 1928. Nor did any of these men do the country or the stock market any harm. They stayed solvent and provided the capital for the next economic upturn.

THE FACTS OF THE CASE

If anyone is still not convinced, the facts are these:

(1)   If there was anything unethical, immoral, illegal, or un-American about it, the Securities and Exchange Commission wouldn't allow it.
(2)   The country cannot benefit from having all its investing citizens lose money. Therefore, if some are able to make money in a declining market, this is all to the good. A free society needs solvent citizens, in order to remain free. One might also say it's a patriotic duty to stay solvent. And, if short selling does that in a bear market, it can hardly be evil. You can't help your family, country, or self if you lose your money.
(3)   Stock prices are merely people's *opinions* of their value. And, since stocks once sold by the company are no longer the property of the company, the shorting of those shares is *not* shorting the company but rather shorting the *opinion* of the company as held by other investors or traders. Microsoft doesn't get your money if you buy its shares, neither does it lose money if you sell its shares short and they drop in price and you make a profit thereby. You merely *won a bet* with a fellow investor. He thought they would go up. You thought not. You won. I'll have more to say in defense of short selling in Chapter 13. It has been misunderstood for decades.
(4)   The short seller contributes mightily to the creation of more orderly and stabilized security markets through the demand for and the supply of securities he creates. In bull markets and bear, he is selling short, and he is eventually "covering" (i.e., buying), which demand puts a cushion under market declines. Without the short seller, our markets would be *bottomless*—those times when panic prevails and bulls rush for the exits while the short seller is calmly buying stock to cover his shorts and taking a profit.

BEAR MARKETS ARE INEVITABLE

It's only reasonable to ask why we have bear markets. Many think we should have progressed far enough in social structure, in government guarantees, floors, and protection that we should have no more depressions, recessions, or bear markets. But to so think is to say we have changed human nature and repealed the law of supply and demand and stopped the pendulum that swings from surplus to insufficiency. Usually when government tries to manipulate prosperity, instead of allowing the business cycle to take its course, they make matters worse. For they destroy the price mechanism that lies at the heart of our free markets' system.

It's what Nobel Laureate F.A. Hayek refers to as the *special information* we all have that causes us to buy or sell at certain prices, but to regard products as too expensive or too cheap at others, which causes shortages or surpluses before the system adjusts.

The business cycle simply reflects evolving markets. But, except in limited situations where liquidity is needed to prevent panic spreading, most government intervention is of little help and over the long term usually makes a situation worse. There are always "unintended consequences" to all government interference in an economy or market.

For hundreds of years, people have been saying, at certain levels of the business cycle, that they were in a "new era of permanent prosperity." Even in ancient Rome, they were under the impression they had a fixed state of affairs—an affluent society—as masters of the world. And, during the 1920s, so convinced was everybody that their new technology had ushered in a New Era that, just weeks before the 1929 crash began a decade-long depression, it was publicly stated that America had entered a permanent plateau of prosperity. "The more things change, the more they remain the same."

No matter what a legislature does, no matter what a President, Prime Minister or Federal Reserve Chairman says, no matter what new concepts are around, the natural cycles of rise and fall take their toll—be it in stock markets, coffee prices, gold, land values, or whatever.

GOING TO EXTREMES

Simply put, a bear market in stocks comes about because the prices get too high in relation to their value. This is caused by public enthusiasm that gradually becomes excessive, appraising stocks out of proportion to their "true" earnings.

It is the nature of such things to go to extremes in both directions. So, as a bull market often goes too high, so too does a bear market go too low. The excesses are caused by human emotions, about which we have more to say in the chapters on human psychology.

THE FALSE PROPHETS

One of the aspects of depressions, recessions, and bear markets that is most difficult to understand is the "false leadership" or false prophets that are prevalent during these times. In part, it's intentionally false, as in the case of most political parties when in office. If they suspect (from government data) the business future is grim, they will rarely reveal this if they can avoid it. And what *must* be revealed to the public is distorted or delayed or colored. This is only human. Nobody wants to lose his or her job, and recessions and depressions usually cause politicians to lose the next election.

The talking heads on television have a vested interest in talking markets up to maintain their station's advertising revenue, and their jobs. Vested interest is knee-deep in the TV and mass media worlds.

False prophets often speak with great sincerity when they say they foresee great prosperity ahead. Or if that statement seems less than realistic, then it's a combination of wishful thinking and self-interest that cause them to announce we will have a "soft landing," that we should be looking for new buying opportunities, that we've made a bottom. Most honestly can't see around the corner. This is no crime. But if one wants to preserve his capital (and perhaps even dare to dream of increasing it) during a sick economy or market period, one must try to see *around the corner*. An important requirement for investment success is to think "contra." If the Secretary of the Treasury in any nation says he looks for next year to be better than this year, one should form the habit of automatically being skeptical. It may be meant as a statement of fact, but the odds are that it isn't. And by doubting it, you prepare yourself for preserving your capital. As Diogenes (325 BC) advises: "Be a cynic."

Likewise, in bad times, the chairman of some board may forecast that software sales will be rather miserable again next year. This should be greeted with the same reaction. It's probably a time to buy shares in software companies. They may be right, but get into the *habit* of thinking they are wrong, because they probably are. The majority usually are. Even the majority of board chairmen, or Treasury Secretaries and Exchequers!

The main focus of this book is help you to think your way to prosperity. I'll offer some formulas, indicators, and strategies. But tools are of limited use if you don't accompany them with logical, nonconformist, contrary thinking—an increasingly lost art in these days of computers and the Internet. Contrary to a computer? Yes, at times.

WHAT CAUSES A DEPRESSION?

Depressions or recessions are caused by basic economic changes of supply or demand or credit. What leaders *say* about circumstances cannot in itself help or hurt the situation, except perhaps for a few days.

Talk just doesn't matter. If an apple is rotten, the act of saying so will not make it ripe. If it's ripe and someone calls it rotten, it will not turn rotten on the spot just because of this characterization.

RECOGNIZING THE BEAR

The final section of this chapter must deal with the recognition of a bear market. How do you know when you are in one? While we will go into more detail in later chapters, one basic approach was defined by Charles H. Dow in a *Wall Street Journal* editorial of July 7, 1900. This premise still holds today. He called it: "The Great Law of Action and Reaction." Today, it is generally known as "the 50% principle."

The sum of what Dow said so many years ago was:

> "It is a remarkable fact in speculation that both the average price of a number of stocks and the price of individual stocks show strong tendencies, both in rallies and relapses, to reach one half of all the primary movement. When a stock falls ten points in a comparatively direct move, it is extremely likely to rally as much as five points from the lowest. It often rallies or relapses more than half of the original swing, but it is generally safe to wait for about half.
>
> "A Comparison of the Averages ... shows how regularly this movement occurs. When a recovery does not come near being one half of a decline, it generally means that the primary movement has not been completed and that a new low quotation will be made."

In Figure 2.1, we see the principle behind Dow's words. If the left end of the beam (marked A) is forced up from its resting position, the beam will approach the horizontal position or 50% level (dotted position B). If the upward thrust has been great enough, the beam will swing all the way up to the high position (dotted position C). But if the upward thrust from A was insufficient, the beam may approach or touch the 50% level (B), falter, and then sink back to the original position at A.

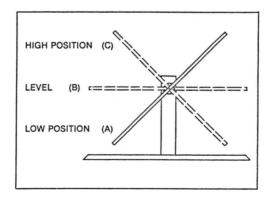

Figure 2.1

TO SUM UP

Thus we might draw these conclusions, based on Dow's idea:

1.   Following a major market advance, if, on the subsequent correction, the (Industrial) Average holds persistently above the halfway (50%) level, the odds favor the highs again being approached (or bettered).
2.   Conversely, following a major advance, if the subsequent retracement or correction goes below the 50% level, the primary direction can be considered to have turned down. The preceding lows may then be approached (or passed).
3.   Following a bear market, if a bull move succeeds in retracing 50% or more of the previous bear market decline, the odds then favor a new bull market's approaching or bettering the old bull market high.
4.   Following a bull market, if the next bear market succeeds in erasing more than 50% of the total bull market gains, the odds then favor the bear market's testing the old bull market low.

This principle applies in many fields, not just the stock market. If what I say in this book applied only to the stock market, it might be valueless because the market is made up of nothing more than people's opinions. What they think and do makes prices move. So, to understand the market, we must also try to understand people and their motivations. We must also factor in social, political, and cultural aspects of human behavior when making a market decision. One must act contrary to the majority view—at the proper time and in the proper way.

A CAUTION

This book is necessarily written at one place in time, and looking ahead is still an inexact science, indeed an art more than a science. You, dear reader, must adjust your thinking as I will adjust mine, day by day, using the methods outlined in these pages.

3
History of Bear Markets

"To be ignorant of what occurred before you were born is to remain forever a child. For what is the worth of human life, unless it is woven into the life of our ancestors by the records of history?"

Cicero, 46 BC

THE USE AND ABUSE OF HISTORY

History never repeats exactly. When we look to history for indicators of what the future might bring, we need to take a "little of this model and a little of that" in order to create a new composite model that is unlike anything that has happened before. This lesson has been forgotten after 20 years of an almost unbroken bull market.

The possibility that we could get a protracted multi-year global bear market and recession is outside the comprehension of most investors.

Most floor traders and fund managers today began their careers after 1980, so have no personal experience of the massive inflationary bear market of the 1970s. And when it began in 1966, many of them were not yet born.

TECHNOLOGY FOSTERS LAZY THINKING

Since the introduction of stock market software, it has become increasingly fashionable to compare today's stock market patterns with past models, without taking into consideration that what created those particular patterns were not just market related but caused by cultural and political factors as well.

Technology has made our lives infinitely more comfortable. But it is a double-edged sword. The more we rely on technology, the less we think for ourselves. And making informed judgments on the future of securities markets, based on an inner sense that comes from working with market data over many years, has become a lost art. Yet, there are so many factors that affect market behavior that cannot be reduced to a software package or a computer-generated predictive system.

In this chapter, we list all bear markets for the last 100 years. But it is up to you, dear reader, to apply the models of history to current and future conditions, using not just market history, but the history of social, political, and economic events for the 20th century.

An in-depth discussion of how these non-market historical events interacted with market action is outside the scope of this book. I therefore suggest you obtain a good year-by-year social history book of the last 100 years, to use in conjunction with this list of past bear markets. You'll find it fun.

TAKING A VIEW

In Europe, where capital preservation is of a higher priority than a quick profit, they are in the habit of "taking a view." While they may trade the intermediate and short-term swings of the market, they do it within the context of a multi-year concept of where the world in general economic terms is heading. This creates a difference between the two continents in how bear markets are defined.

In America, all bear markets tend to be given equal ranking, with no consideration to the bigger picture. But that limited view is not particularly helpful for the longer term investor, particularly in today's investment climate. I will elaborate on how "taking a view" applies to the next few years in Chapter 19. But, in this chapter on bear market history, let us concentrate only on the past.

In the last 70 years, there have been two major occasions when taking a view enabled you to see a different, more accurate picture of events, than simply treating every uptrend in the market as a bull market, and every down-leg as a bear.

These periods are 1929 to 1942, and from 1966 to 1982. Both periods were times when there were major economic and monetary problems that took well over a decade to resolve. Both periods were mirror images of what we have experienced between 1982 and 2000.

On an economic and financial level, those 18 years have been a time of considerable growth. This gave rise to an almost continuous bull market. The mini-bear markets of 1987 and 1990 were almost exclusively Wall Street phenomena, in that little or no damage was done to the economic and financial health of the companies, which stocks represent. The *major* uptrend remained intact. But the long-term investor, who did not sell out before August 1987, found himself with major losses just 2 months later. And, by October, there was a lot of panic selling. But the investor who "took a view" would have known that October 1987 was not the time to sell.

However, if that same long-term investor had looked at the underlying financial and economic structure in the late 1960s, he would have seen that not only was there a "bubble" mentality in electronics stocks, but that there were profound fiscal problems which were eating away at the economic health of American companies. This ultimately led to double-digit inflation. A new major bull market did not begin until the inflation was squeezed out of the economy.

Between 1929 and 1932, the economy sustained tremendous economic damage. Even though the Dow rose 268% over the next 5 years, the damage caused to the economy and the dollar was not resolved until 1942. Thereafter, a sustained bull market began, which did not end until 1966.

My point is that the simplistic conventional definitions of bear markets, that simply measure the extent of the drop in the various Averages in some sort of ratio to the time it takes for the drop to occur, are not very helpful to an investor deciding whether to unload his stocks at a loss, or hold on in hopes they will go back to their old highs.

This doesn't mean that one should have gotten out of stocks in early 1929 or 1966 and taken a holiday from the stock market for the next decade or so, although some people did. Instead, it means that when your "taking a view" indicators tell you that there are major economic and monetary problems that are likely to take a year or more to be resolved, you no longer can buy and hold, but should become a more watchful and flexible investor, playing the major upmoves, but doing so with one hand on the exit all the way up.

I belabor this point because as of this writing, in early 2002, some analysts are predicting the beginning of a new bull market. I do not necessarily disagree with them. The Dow Jones Industrial Average or S&P Average could retrace much of their losses since 2000. If they do, they will do so with little regard for the global economic and monetary problems that began long before the September 11 attack, and will be there for some time to come.

The cry of those proclaiming a new bull market is that the market generally leads the economy by 3–6 months. So, if we are in a new bull market, that must mean economic problems will be solved in 2002. That displays a faulty knowledge of history. The major bull market in the 1930s, and the two major bull markets during the 1970s, did not herald an end to the underlying monetary problems. Quite the reverse. In all cases, it was the lack of solution to the underlying health of the economy that pulled the markets back down.

Why should we take a view and not treat all bear markets as equal?

An example of this wrong thinking is the comparison of 1987 to the crash phase of 1929. Many people believe the Federal Reserve single-handedly prevented 1987 from becoming another 1929. Ergo, we now know enough to prevent another major bear market and depression of the 1930s magnitude. But if Fed intervention, which worked so well in 1987, is the way to prevent all future bear markets, why is it that since 2000, after more aggressive cutting of the discount rate by the Fed than at any time in history, there has been no 1987 style turnaround?

1987 AND 1929 COMPARED

- After a 6-year bull market, beginning in 1923, the DJIA more than quadrupled, reaching an all-time high on September 3, 1929. The DJIA lost 40% during the next 55 days. In a selling climax on October 28 and 29, 1929, the DJIA lost 20% in just 2 days.
- After sustained growth which began in 1984, the DJIA had almost tripled its low point of 3 years earlier. The Dow reached its peak of 2,722.42 on August 25, 1987.
- The 1987 crash phase, as with 1929, began 55 days after the late summer high.
- From peak to trough, the 1987 market lost 36.1% of its value, compared to 39.6% on the first leg in 1929.

For somebody who did not "take a view" but looked only at the numbers, it appeared that 1929 and 1987 were similar bear markets. Those investors who, in 1987, believed they were seeing a rerun of 1929 came to two different and equally wrong conclusions. One group believed that 1987 was the beginning of a 1930s-style bear market, so missed out on much of the bull market which followed. The other group saw the Federal Reserve as a kind of latter-day Merlin, capable of creating permanent prosperity out of a potential 1929 situation. This latter group are still wondering why the recent, most aggressive rate cutting in history didn't pull the same rabbit out of the hat that it did in 1987.

As Mark Twain said: "There are lies, damn lies, and statistics."

The ability of computers to crunch numbers faster and better than ever before is a wonderful advance. But it has its drawbacks.

The good side is that computers can process numbers and find connections that previously was impossible. The bad side is that ever more reliance on computers causes people to think ever less. And investing requires thinking. It is not a lazy man's hobby.

THE BEAR'S RECORD BOOK

The first step to creating that composite model to see what the future may look like is to glance over past bear markets. You'll find this of great help as reference material in the years to come (and especially for all the bear markets ahead).

No single past model exactly applies to today.

My list begins in 1900, because this was the first bear market after Dow created the DJIA in 1897. Panics and crashes from earlier times also have things they can teach us, but prior to 1897 market statistics are vague, so anything earlier can only be referred to in a general sense:

1900   DJIA declined 31.8%. Duration of bear market: 12 months. Crash came in December 1899. Bear market low in June 1900.

1903   DJIA declined 37.7%. Duration: 10 months. Crash occurred in November 1902. Bear market low in September 1903.

1907   DJIA declined 45.0%. Duration: 10 months. Had two crash phases, the first in February (DJIA fell 21.8% in this first phase); rallied in March and April.

The second crash was July to November, a 4-month fall known historically as the "Panic of 1907." A bull market started at once after the second crash. Stocks lost almost 50% (many much more) from the bull peak. A further fall was prohibited by the fact that business did not fall much further after the October economic collapse. Business coasted in a top area for 8 months after the start of the first market crash, then, suddenly and without an alarm, plunged down almost vertically in the midst of the second market crash.

Business indicators hit bottom 3 months later, stayed there for 4 months, then began a healthy recovery:

1909   DJIA declined 26.2%. Started in November 1909, with the crash phase in February 1910. The bear market low came in July 1910. Duration: 8 months.

1912   DJIA declined 23.5%. Duration of bear market: 26 months. Crash came in June 1913, but bear had started in November 1912. Bear low came in December 1914. Since the stock market was closed for 4 months in 1914 by the war, a true picture of the decline here is impossible. One source says it was 36.3%. But I'll take the more conservative published DJIA figures as my base.

1917   DJIA declined 40.1%. Duration of bear market: 13 months. Crash phase came in December 1916. Hit bear market low in December 1917.

1919   DJIA declined 46.6%. Duration: 21 months. Three crash phases. Initial crash November 1919 to February 1920 (DJIA fell 25% in this first phase). Second crash in late 1920. Final crash in summer of 1921. Hit low in June.

Business topped out slowly during the first market crash, then coasted rather indecisively just below its top area for 6 months after the crash. Then it plunged sharply, right after Labor Day, 1920. A depression lasting 1 year followed. Business then recovered simultaneously with the stock market. The year 1921 was notable for a downswing that lasted 6 months nonstop, the second longest downswing in bear market history.

1923   DJIA declined 18.6%. Duration of this baby bear market: 7 months.
1926   DJIA declined 16.6%. Duration of baby bear market: 2 months.
1929   DJIA declined 90.0%. Duration 34 months. Six successive market crashes comprised this famed bear: (1) September to November 1929 (DJIA fell 40% in this first phase). (2) April to June 1930. (3) September to December 1930. (4) March to May 1931. (5) July to January 1932. (6) March to July 1932. A new bull market then started immediately, as did a business recovery.

Business had topped out mildly, a month before the first crash; a gradual mild decline continued to April 1930, then fell sharply into a depression simultaneously with the end of the 1930 stock market rally. The business decline halted in December 1930, stayed level for 6 months, then plunged again in steep economic decline that didn't lose its downward momentum for a full year, until July 1932. Business improved intermittently thereafter but still remained at depression levels through most of the 1930s except for a short recovery in 1936–37.

1934   Rarely included among bear markets. But a fall of 24.1% in the DJIA gives it a deserved berth here. Duration: 9 months. Then the market took seven more months to get back up to where 1934 began.
1937   DJIA declined 51.8%. Duration: 56 months. Five crash phases: (1) August to November (DJIA fell 40% in this first phase). (2) February to March 1938. (3) January to April 1939. (4) May 1940. (5) October 1941 to April 1942. Business peaked out and fell violently, simultaneously with stocks. Economic indicators bottomed out 9 months later (May 1938). The recovery began mildly at first, but was later boosted by the World War II production boom which eventually lifted the country out of the Great Depression of the 1930s.

The period 1941–42 contained the longest bear market nonstop downswing ($7\frac{1}{2}$ months) in history. Certain analysts call this two separate bear markets, one from September 1937 to March 1938, and the second from May 1940 to April 1942. If you are simply looking at market action this view may be correct. But if you take a wider view within the context of the depressed mood of the times, then it can be viewed as all part of a single bear market.

1946 DJIA declined 24.6%. Duration: 37 months. There was only one crash phase (August–September 1946), and the bottom was hit within 4 months. But the market moved sideways for almost three years and tested the 1946 low area three times. The final time was in 1949, after which the market rose almost without interruption for the next 12 years (160 to 741 in 1961).

1953 This was a very small bear market, but, as it was caused by war (Korea) uncertainty, I include it here. DJIA declined 13.9% (295 to 254). Duration of this quasi-bear market: 9 months.

1957 DJIA plummeted 106 points (522 to 416) for a 20.3% fall. Duration: 6 months.

1960 Opinions differ on whether this was a real bear market. But Dow Theory signals were given, so it is included here. DJIA declined 18.0%. Points lost: 124. Duration: 10 months.

1962 DJIA declined 29% in 6 months. Extent of 1962 damage: the first crash phase of 1929 lost 40 billion dollars. The 1962 crash lost over 100 billion dollars. Even if we adjust those values in terms of 1929 purchasing power, the 1962 crash still lost one and a quarter times as much as in 1929.

1966 Market plunged from 1001 to 735 in just over 8 months. This was the end of the postwar super-bull market. At this point, the whole atmosphere of the stock market changed. A new factor entered the investor's reasoning. Not only must he now assess the direction of the economy, he must also consider government monetary intervention, which might make him think he was making a profit, when in fact, in real value terms, he was not. We will discuss this at greater length in Chapter 19.

1968 This was a long, drawn-out bear market. The DJIA declined from a high in December 1968 of 994, down to a low of 627 in May 1970. This was the first of the new-era bear markets, caused not so much by a simple downturn in business but by currency woes.

1973 This one was scary! From a high of 1067 in January 1973, the market slid relentlessly down to its final low of 570 in December 1974. Its catalyst was the oil crisis. For the first time in American stock market history, a foreign power, or group of powers, were able to precipitate an economic slowdown. We had entered a new level of globalization after which the world would never be the same.

1977 DJIA fell fairly gradually, though gathering some momentum as it went from just over 1000 in January 1977 to a low of 736 in March 1978. Nothing dramatic caused it; rather more of the same of the past decade: increasing oil prices with dollar stability problems steadily worsening.

1981   This bear snuck up on people. DJIA made a rare quadruple top that convinced most investors it was building strength to break through. DJIA fell from 1025 in April 1981 to a low of 770 in August 1982, or 255 points. A mere 17-month-long bear, it led to a recession which was more severe than the stock market fall would indicate.

1984   Though this is not even considered a bear market by most, it scared a lot of investors because it broke below a giant support area and appeared to be heading back to the 1000 level, whence the bull market of late 1982 and all of 1983 had come. It fell 16%, from 1295 to 1080 in 7 months.

1987   This was a heart-stopper for the very reason that there was no apparent economic reason for it to occur. There were two catastrophic days of multi-hundred point drops, with one of those days being the largest one-day point drop in history. It came about because of computer programming (explained earlier), computer insurance schemes, and the globalization of markets. It was history's first simultaneous global bear market where all major world markets were hit badly at the same time. Australia was among the hardest hit, Japan among the least, but all had considerable damage. DJIA fell from 2747 to 1616 (i.e., 36.1%), in less than 2 months. It took nearly 2 years to surpass its prior high.

1990   This was the direct result of Iraq invading Kuwait, and was halted when the US launched Desert Storm. DJIA declined 17%. Duration: 4 months. This bear market, along with that of 1987 are the shortest bear markets in history.

2000   By October 2001, the Nasdaq was down a whopping 72% though the DJIA was only down around 25%. But most worrying, well before the September 11, 2001 terrorist attack, was that the underlying economic health of the US and most world economies showed increasing signs of weakness. It is already clear that this bear market has damaged the broader economic health of all major economies, more than any other bear market in the last 60 years. But more of this later in our predictions chapter.

BEAR MARKET FREQUENCY RATIO

So, there you have the bear markets of the 20th century, and the first one of the 21st century. There has been a bear market every 4 years on average. The longest time span between bear markets has been the most recent bull market, which was 10 years if you regard 1990 as a major bear market; 20 years if you "take a view."

This is the powerful message, then, of this chapter: that even if you weight all bear markets as equal, and don't think in terms of multi-decade papa bear markets within which mama and baby bull markets are possible, bear markets are frequent enough to make it impossible to ignore them, even in major boom times, or to avoid their losses.

The decade of the 1990s was unique and, like the bear markets of 1987 and 1990, occurred because of a unique set of circumstances that are unlikely to repeat, let alone be considered a new paradigm for bull markets in the future— at least not in our lifetimes.

Thus, the investor must try to understand bear markets better. Otherwise, the profits from the previous bull market are usually wiped out.

AVERAGE PERCENTAGE OF VALUE LOSSES

You have also seen that the percentage of decline in bear markets ranges from as little as 13.9% up to 90%. The total of all these percentage losses is phenomenal. The losses represented by all these declines are staggering, but when you realize that the blue-chip averages never fall as far as the great mass of small cap stocks, the damage to your wealth during a bear market can be more than most people can deal with. The averages mask a greater percentage fall by the majority of stocks *not* in the averages.

Add to that the economic and fiscal damage that often accompanies a bear market. Say you lose your job, and that small stock portfolio was your "safety net." Or you needed that extra money for the kid's college fund, or an unexpected illness. You can be sure that the kid's education or sickness in the family won't only occur when your stocks have recovered any losses they might have suffered in the prior bear market.

Unfortunately, during the 1990s, people came to regard investing in stocks as like putting their money in the bank, except that many were making 30% per year instead of bank interest of 5%.

LENGTH OF BEAR MARKETS

Bear markets have been as short as 2 months and as long as 5 years, the average being about 18 months. This current bear is already the longest in 60 years, which of itself suggests that although we may see what many analysts call a new bull market, it will more likely resemble those baby bulls of the 1930s and 1970s than the major bull market of the 1990s.

Also, it should be noted that, in the 20th century, markets were in a bear phase for 341 months (i.e., *28 years of bear markets*), and, in the last 90 years, we have been in bear markets *35% of the time*. If that statistic doesn't change your belief in a buy and hold investment strategy, nothing will.

Clearly, this makes the stock market a dangerous place—with a pitfall hidden under every third stepping stone.

Not only does it mean the permanently bullish investor only has two chances in three at best, but when you consider that the depressed psychological climate at bear market bottoms prevents the majority from investing at the best time, it means that, by the time the majority of investors recognize a bull market is present, it is half-gone.

But by showing you how to face bear markets with confidence, and make money in them, I hope that, by the end of this book, you will be among the *first* people to invest in the next great bull market.

TRUE RISKS ARE STAGGERING

The situation is made worse by the fact that the average investor (90% of investors) can't be expected to spot the exact top of bull markets and sell out in time. This means he loses much of the prior rise before he does sell. A professional man, a physician, who throughout the late 1990s prided himself on his ability to trade online, admitted to me a few months ago that: "I haven't sold anything because what would I do with the money?"

Then, a month after the September 11 attack, he remarked that it was only on October 1 (i.e., 3 weeks after the attack) that he had the courage to switch on his computer to check the prices of his stocks! His reactions, which I am sure were echoed by millions of investors across America, surely explode the myth that you can just invest and sit and wait.

Everybody needs a plan, one that includes strategies for selling as well as buying—and (once understood) for selling short when that seems to be the prudent course of action. Without a plan of action, when the unexpected occurs, when markets suddenly fall, or terrorist attacks strike, that is not the time to think up an investment strategy. It is a time to act on realistic strategies for both bull and bear markets that you had already decided upon, when you were feeling less stressed.

PERIOD OF READJUSTMENT

For those who still believe that if they hold on they will do better than if they sell at a loss, let me reveal another statistic. After each of the 21 bear markets prior to 1987, prices did not immediately zoom back to new high ground. This "V" bottom, that analysts always tell you they are expecting shortly, has absolutely no history in prior bear markets that have gone on over 18 months, as this one has. Most of those 21 bear markets took many months or even years to get back to where they were before the fall.

After the 1929 bear, it took *26 years* to recover. If that is too extreme or too much like ancient history to you, it took *14 years* after the 1937 crash, and the 1966 peak of 995.15 was not decisively breached on the upside until 1982 (i.e., *16 years* later). And, along the way, there were some pretty wild swings to the downside including the 1974 low when the DJIA lost nearly 50% of its value, and in ever more inflated (depreciating) dollars. So to buy and hold, you not only need lots of patience, lots of spare cash (so you won't need to draw on your investments to pay bills), but you also need nerves of steel to sit through the decline.

LEARNING FROM THE PAST

> "I saw a new heaven and a new earth ... and the former things were unremembered."

This seems to be true of every age. In 1929, they had had seven prior bear markets, just since 1900, on which to build their knowledge. But it was to no avail. People, by nature, almost defy learning from the past. They contend that having had depressions, man acts to prevent their recurrence. But the evidence doesn't support this.

Militaries usually focus on better ways to fight the *last* war, that's why when terrorists used a passenger plane as a megaton bomb, not only was the military totally unprepared to deal with such an attack, but Intelligence (which is supposed to find out about these things before they happen) had no idea such an attack was imminent. Both military and Intelligence were focused on possible terrorist use of smart bombs à la the Gulf War, or nuclear devices.

So too with many economists and market analysts, who compile the data from past bear markets, and then search current market conditions for an exact match with past models. Any future bear market will be sufficiently unique and there will be sufficient "proof" that this bear does not fit any prior model, to enable people to deny that it is happening all the way into bankruptcy.

CONCLUSION

If a conclusion is possible, it is probably that the only way to avoid odds that are little different from red and black in roulette, is to play both sides of the wheel (i.e., be willing to hold stocks long or short (or both) as circumstances warrant). You should have contingency plans in place if markets don't act as you expected, and use what economists call "unarticulated knowledge," but which the rest of us call intuition: that inner judgment that takes into account social, political, and cultural conditions, often without bringing it to your conscious attention except in the form of an uneasy feeling. Be flexible and trust your instincts.

Part II
ECONOMIC SETTING FOR BEAR MARKETS

"Ultimately, in a free society, we cannot protect people from all the consequences of their own errors. We cannot protect people completely without denying them the possibility of achieving their own fulfillment. We cannot completely protect society from the effects of waves of irrational exuberance or irrational pessimism—emotional reactions that are themselves part of the human condition."

Irrational Exuberance, by Robert J. Shiller,
Princeton University Press, 2000

4
Guideposts for Bear Markets

"It requires a great deal of boldness and a great deal of caution to make a great fortune, and when you have got it, it requires ten times as much wit to keep it."

Ralph Waldo Emerson (1803–82)

Lists of data abound, showing signs to look for to tip you off as to whether we're heading for business improvement or slump, or for a bull or bear market. During the latter part of the 1990s, these data was used *selectively* by financial commentators. Analysts fought to get air time or print space for self-serving reasons. And Wall Street became part of the entertainment industry.

Thoughtful judgment calls, based on extensive research, were no longer expected of TV or print media analysts. Instead, they were and are expected to entertain viewers and readers, and to put a *positive spin* on all economic and financial data, no matter how dire it is in reality.

Market terminology is being twisted into the new language of Street-Speak, where nothing is ever what it seems, and the need for news has disappeared in favor of the need to be reassured that, no matter what happens, the bull market will resume next week or next month.

Symbols have taken over from substance. And after years of the Clinton-induced culture of "feeling your pain," a major reaction in the US to the September 11, 2001 attack was to go out and buy a flag and wallow in the emotions of grief, instead of learning about crisis management for their portfolios, responsible citizenship, and for their daily lives.

My first book in 1964 was also on bear markets. In it, I published a list of "bear market signs" for the responsible investor to watch, to alert them when a bear market was imminent. Though many of those signs are still valid for a medium and long-term investor, and I will get to them in a moment, the way many of them now operate has changed drastically in the last 5 years. Until about 1995, technical indicators usually had a few weeks lag time before the data manifested themselves in the markets. And the connection between economic conditions and stock market direction was still accepted as fact.

But, from about 1995 on, the media and governments have manipulated all data so much that the average investor today believes that, provided the Federal Reserve and US government cut interest rates or create bail-out packages, it won't be long before the late great bull market of the 1990s resumes.

Even the language has changed. In the 1980s, when it was necessary to subsidize the Savings and Loan industry to prevent it from collapsing, it was called a "bail-out." And, though it did not cause a full-blown bear market, it was considered bearish enough to create a sizable correction in the DJIA. In late 2001, with the airline industry on the verge of collapse and production at new lows, the bail-out was called "an economic stimulus package," and investors' reaction to the news has been to push the market back up!

In the past, increased government spending and, at the same time, massive increases in the money supply were regarded as fiscally irresponsible and a harbinger of inflation. Today, investors turn to government with the same naive gratitude a small boy might show a parent who replaced the pocket money he lost.

The media has created a culture of victim investors: when the news is negative but not "our fault." The media admits there are problems but blame it on terrorists or whoever. But when the news is positive it is the government who claims the credit for creating that success.

This causes far more volatility in markets than ever before because, when the only factors admitted to be causing a business turndown are claimed to come from outside, markets seem totally unpredictable and people will panic more.

But none of this has changed the laws of economics, or stock markets. And companies "patriotically" and foolishly buying back their own stock or investors watching their retirement accounts diminish while they wave the flag won't change long-term trends, nor do a thing to solve the very real problems that the economy had long before September 11, 2001.

During the near vertical fall in 1930, John D. Rockefeller consumed a considerable portion of his enormous fortune buying back his stock in Standard Oil, then a DJIA company. He managed to stall the market fall for a few days. But he was no more able to reverse the laws of economics than today's "patriotic" investors can.

What has been totally forgotten in the last several years is that when Charles Dow created his Average, he saw it, not as a stock market indicator, but as an indicator of *economic* health. He understood that stocks are no better or worse than the companies they represent. It is the economy that drives the stock market, not the other way round. Yet today, the only time commentators admit the connection between the price of stocks and the companies they represent is when there is a technical rally in stocks, and they remind us that stocks rise before a recession is ended. Ergo, if stocks rise, the economic recovery must be just a few weeks away.

SIGNS A BULL MARKET IS ENDING

No matter what Washington or the media claim, bull markets cannot be sustained if the economy is faltering. Neither can a bear market suddenly become a new bull market, with a "V" bottom (media-speak) while economic indicators are getting weaker:

1. The most important indicator that a downturn still has a long way to go is when investor sentiment is still bullish while the underlying economic structure continues to weaken.

2. Price earnings ratios. In recent years, even rational analysts have puzzled over why they no longer seem to "work." This is all part of the separation of stocks from the values of the companies they represent. In his book *Irrational Exuberance*, Yale professor Robert Shiller points out that, since 1870, price earnings ratios for big companies have averaged just under 13 for a yield of 7.75%. In late 2001, that ratio was between 25 and 35, for a yield of about 2–4%, depending which biased source you read. To return to a more traditional price earnings ratio, the DJIA would have to fall to at least 5000. I will discuss that in more detail in a later chapter, but suffice it to say here that it suggests that this bear market has further to fall.

3. The Federal Reserve. Fed action has been the most closely watched indicator in the last 5 years. But, with the most aggressive rate reductions in history, driving US interest rates down to a level not seen since the 1960s and with no result, it is increasingly clear that when the US economy goes south, there is little government can do to stop it.

4. Consumer and Investor Confidence. There is always an abundance of confidence in the future of business and the market, at peaks. Even after markets turn down, as long as that confidence remains high the bear market has further to go. Markets traditionally turn around on low volume in the middle of widespread gloom about the future. Those who buy at the very beginning of major bull markets or sell at the beginning of bear markets are regarded as equally unhinged, as I was regarded in the Spring of 2000 when I suggested, in my newsletter, the Nasdaq was a sell.

5.   Gold. In times of uncertainty, the interest in gold and gold shares picks up.

6.   Real Estate. It is normal for real estate prices to rise with stock market prices. There is usually a lot of public speculation in real estate at bull market tops. Whether real estate turns down in a bear market depends on how much inflation there is. In inflationary bear markets, real estate is seen as a haven and prices rise. In bear markets where inflation is low and the currency firm, real estate prices will usually stay firm in the early stages, but will decline as the bear market deepens.

7.   Stock market action. At tops, there is what is commonly classified as "churning" (i.e., high volume but not much change in prices, or great irregularity in prices [some up sharply, some down sharply], plus a lot of volatility day to day).

8.   Unanimity of bullish forecasts. Business leaders, brokers, advisory services, columnists and broadcasters are, in the main, bullish. Any downturn is dismissed as temporary.

9.   Sharp rise in debt. At the top of a bull market, the pervasive mood is that one can make a profit in markets, without risk. Consumer debt, household debt service payments, losses by credit card issuers, bankruptcy filings and mortgage delinquencies all rise sharply.

This list is not complete and, with government playing an ever bigger role in our financial and economic lives, this list changes constantly. But I offer this list to stimulate your own thinking, as an antidote to the pap coming from the media and government trying to convince you that if you just buy and hold, consume like crazy, and put your trust in government, the economy will roll as it did in the 1990s.

I encourage you to be ever mindful of how free markets work, and that the basis of prosperity is responsible citizens willing to assume risk, who never lose sight of the fact that all monetary decisions involve risk. Our system relies on solvent citizens who are self-reliant, not on government's ability to manipulate interest rates or create "stimulus packages."

FADS AS A LEADING INDICATOR FOR THE END OF A BULL MARKET

All major bull markets of the last 100 years were fueled by new technology. But, in most instances, the genuine advances that the technology created were exaggerated into what became an almost religious belief in technology for its own sake. New Eras and New Economies became fads.

Toward the end of bull markets, fads increase and give us a hint of our nearness to the next bear market. Both fads and new technological advances look much the same on the surface. Experience brings the ability to tell the difference between "the sizzle and the steak."

Thus, in the 17th century, when the big tulip craze hit, a savvy investor with a modicum of common sense should have suspected that, however full of limitless possibilities the new globalization that enabled the Dutch to enjoy this exotic flower was, a single tulip bulb could not possibly be worth the price of an Amsterdam house. But hundreds of experienced investors bought tulips as symbols of the new shipping technology, rather than buying tulips on their own merits. They bought into a fad. So it was in the 1920 Florida land craze.

There was nothing wrong with either Holland's tulips or Florida's land. But one needs to look at them as business propositions, instead of getting caught up in an abstract idea.

Investment trusts (we call them Mutual Funds now) were a fad before the 1929 crash. In the late 1960s, it was electronics companies, many of which by 1970 had lost 80% of their earlier value, and some had gone out of business entirely. We saw a similar fad in the late 1990s in the form of dot.coms. Both electronics and the Internet have been magnificent technological advances, and we will enjoy their benefits for years to come. But they became fads because they represented such spectacular advances that investors ignored such mundane considerations of whether the companies using the technology were viable businesses. Fads are a major indicator that a bull market is reaching a bubble stage.

SIGNS A BEAR MARKET IS ENDING

1. Bad news abundant. The stock market always seems to start up before the bad news (about lower industrial production, unemployment, lack of consumer confidence, etc.) stops. At that point, the market will be acting "contrary to the obvious," which is usually a good sign that the market is right in whatever it does.

2. Credit. Still tight. But credit balances in brokerage accounts usually are considerable. Large holdings in bonds and other cash-related investments. This latent buying power is what will give a new bull market its stamina.

3. Stock Market. Volume low, not much interest. Stocks selling at low price earnings ratios, high yields. But then new lows in the DJIA and S&P occur on even lower volumes. Some key stocks begin to show good rally potential. Volume tends to increase on rallies, decrease on dips. *Charts* are the way to spot this.

4. Confidence. Nil. Pessimistic forecasts made for the market and for business.

5.   Real Estate. Unless it has been an inflationary bear market, real estate prices will be down. It is hard to sell property. Lots of empty commercial buildings. Rents reduced. Foreclosures rise.

6.   Bonds. Government bond buying is popular. Corporate bonds are high, yields low.

THREE BEAR PHASES

It may shed further light here to quote from Robert Rhea, who was a hugely successful investment advisor during the 1930s. I will quote a number of market researchers from the 1930s and 1940s in this book because they saw things a lot more clearly than many do today. Government and media spin was not in vogue, then.

Today, in our highly complex world, we tend to lose sight of the forest because we are too busy avoiding the trees and the undergrowth. Writers from a simpler time had the luxury of being able to see the big picture with less distractions from "clutter." Today, TV sound bites appeal and deceive simultaneously. Said Rhea:

> "Bear markets seem to be divided into three phases: the first being the abandonment of hopes upon which the uprush of the preceding bull market was predicated; the second being the reflection of the decreased earning power and reduction of dividends; and the third representing distress liquidation of securities which must be sold to meet living expenses. Each of these phases seems to be divided by a secondary reaction which is often erroneously assumed to be the beginning of a bull market."

WATCH YOUR EMOTIONS

Logan Pearsal Smith, in 1931, said: "Solvency is entirely a matter of temperament and not of income."

My greatest caution in this entire signs-of-the-times section is to urge that you hold a strong rein on yourself, otherwise your emotions or prejudices of the moment (be they bullish or bearish) will cause you to read the total situation as bullish or bearish on the basis of selective evidence. Or, you will be too demanding and expect *too many* signs of the times to be convinced the climate has changed.

BE FIRST

The great advantage of being aware of these potential signs of coming events is that, when you read or hear data of the changing economy, you are able to interpret it immediately and, if necessary, act on it. You know what to look for and you recognize it before it is fully reflected in stock market prices.

If the signs of the times were easily interpreted, the future would be plain for all to see. They aren't, and it isn't.

Don't expect to see too many signs occur at once. They show up over a period of perhaps many months, as the giant economy slowly rolls over, or yawns and slowly comes back to life.

In this respect, we see again that the stock market is non-accommodating. It isn't going to conveniently flash all its red or green lights at once so everyone can see at a glance what direction is next. Remember the old Wall Street adage: "Don't confuse brains with a bull market." And don't imagine that markets turn on dimes and change direction overnight, as the mass media would have you believe.

BUSINESS INDICATORS

Many of the "signs" given earlier in this chapter are business indicators. But the lists are by no means complete. I encourage you to add new signs to your personal list, things which you feel offer keys to a change in market direction.

Many accepted leading indicators are lagging or coincident indicators, so, if you want to stay ahead of the crowd, you need take note of those indicators as soon as the facts are known.

The best way to use these indicators is not to create some mathematical model on your computer (though that's OK as a reminder and checklist) but to develop an internal model in your head. Ideally, make lists of the facts as soon as you know them, with a note of what they will do to what economic indicator and when that indicator will be released, and then forget about it. Slowly, a pattern will emerge without you being conscious of it. Suddenly, you will find yourself muttering "meaningless" when somebody tries to point out the significance of a minor rise in retail sales, or a fall in commodity prices, because of the overall "index" you keep in your head.

To separate wheat from chaff is a vital function amid the signs of the times.

It is a fact that no two bear or bull markets are exactly the same in their manifestations. This is why a single investment software package is of limited use. Software, unlike the human mind, can only compare present models to those in the past, usually almost exactly. And, though we may have a future bear market as inflationary as those in the 1970s, or as economically devastating as the 1930s, or any in-between, the only certainty is that any future bear market will not look exactly like any in the past, though it will doubtless have elements of past markets.

However, software that records and keeps technical indicators for you can be of tremendous value, and saves you the tedium of having to calculate the indicators on a daily or weekly basis.

The type of lateral thinking needed to use the past to construct a plausible future is something that only a human mind can do, and for the foreseeable future no computer can.

THE EFFECTS OF GLOBALIZATION

Today, the world is so interconnected that the economic problems of any nation spills over to every other nation. Everybody exports to everybody else, so when one economy contracts, all those who do business with the problem economy are affected.

You may have no interest in investing outside your own country. But you cannot afford to ignore what is happening in other countries. Economic problems abroad can be a leading indicator of possible problems at home. Even if you never plan to invest in another country, I urge US readers to watch European news on television, and take a subscription to the *Financial Times* and *The Economist*. European media give international coverage of the sort that US media do not. Likewise, non-US readers should read the *New York Herald Tribune* and/or the *Wall Street Journal* for a US insight.

THE HOUSE OF CARDS EFFECT

In our interdependent world, it's a house of cards no matter how you stack it. We stand together or fall together.

For those still not convinced, let me offer an example.

Envisage a major city with several thousand businesses. In a depression, can you imagine that the depression would affect only half of them? Would you expect to find 1,000 prospering as never before while the rest were losing business? Or is it more logical that all would feel the pinch, in varying degrees, of the national slowdown in business?

Today, the global economy functions much like a major city. "Pockets of prosperity" amidst adversity, be they cities, neighborhoods or entire nations, have become rare.

5
Globalization, Terrorism, and Foreign Investment

"A traveler without knowledge is a bird without wings."

Sa'di, *Gulistan* (1258)

In the last 20 years, a number of foreign funds came into being, and conventional wisdom was that a portion of a well-diversified portfolio should be invested in other countries.

Has terrorism changed this idea?

Will the world now revert to a 1930s' mentality of barriers against trade? Answer: globalization is too far advanced to be reversed by terrorism. Europe has lived with terrorism for over 40 years without it unduly affecting their securities and bond markets. It is likely that Wall Street will be the same.

Though events like September 11, 2001 directly affect markets over the short term, what moves markets over the medium and long term are the underlying economics. Those economics may indeed be affected by political actions, ideologies, or acts of terrorism and war. But these non-economic factors will only modify or amplify economic trends already in progress. They will not, unless they are exceptionally severe, reverse them.

During the late great bull market, many American analysts suggested that a well-diversified portfolio should be as much as 50% in foreign investments and 50% in American securities.

In today's highly unstable world, 40–60% would be wiser. There are some foreign investments that come into their own in bear markets. And, in some kinds of bear market, you can make more money investing abroad than you can make investing domestically.

But you should take very seriously the quote at the start of this chapter. If you have little knowledge of a country, study their market charts. Charts *are* knowledge.

Buying and selling foreign stock directly is a bit complicated until you get familiar with the way the issuing country operates. You can check if the shares are available via American Depository Receipts (ADRs). Or use a country fund (e.g., all Japan shares, or all Europe, etc.).

ADRs

An American Depository Receipt is a receipt for shares of a foreign company, deposited in an American bank. Once the initial transaction has been made, a bank issues the ADR, and thereafter those foreign shares trade in much the same way as any American shares do. ADRs are traded only in the US and not on the exchange of the country in which the shares are issued.

For this reason, although the price of an ADR closely follows that of the stock it represents in its country of origin, there is sometimes a fraction of a point difference between the two, which very sophisticated traders use for arbitrage.

Only major non-US companies are available in the form of ADRs. But for the average bear market investor who wants to buy non-US gold mining shares, or shares in any major foreign corporation, ADRs are a handy way to do so.

GOLD MINING SHARES

Some of the best gold mining companies are not American, but Canadian, Australian, or South African. In times of instability, gold mining companies tend to rise ahead of gold bullion, so gold mining shares are often a more attractive buy in the early stages of a bear market, particularly an inflationary bear market. Most major foreign gold mining companies have ADRs.

CURRENCY PLAYS

Another reason to invest abroad during a bear market is if you fear inflation will erode the value of your own currency. The late 1970s was such a time. If you simply want to put money abroad in a foreign currency at interest, the easiest way to do that is via a Swiss or Dutch bank. Swiss and Dutch banks are more internationally minded than most and cater to English-speaking foreign investors. They can set you up with time deposits or bonds for any major currency in the world. How do you open a foreign bank account? Answer: in exactly the same way you open a local account. You either mail your bank of choice a check with instructions to open an account for you, or you make a direct bank transfer. Some major Swiss banks require a minimum deposit in at least six figures, and a few private banks require at least a million dollars. So, check out the bank of your choice before you decide to open an account with them. But the majority will take a minimum $25,000 deposit.

There are US branches of many major foreign banks where you can open your account in person. But, if you seek privacy, avoid them and deal direct.

In any future inflationary bear market of the kind we saw during the 1970s then a Dutch or Swiss bank account would be a good investment move. Will inflation get as bad as it did in the 1970s in the foreseeable future? You will have to wait till Chapter 19 to find out!

You can also trade currency futures on the International Monetary Market (IMM) in Chicago. Futures of any kind are for nimble traders. But it's a skill like all others. It also demands time to monitor, more so than stocks or bonds. Margin requirements for futures are much lower than for stocks, so when you buy a future (in anything, not just a currency future), you are much more leveraged than when you buy a stock, even if you buy a stock on margin. This means if you are correct on the direction of a particular currency, then your profits are multiplied because of the leverage. But if you are wrong, you can lose dramatically. And because bear markets tend to be more volatile than bull markets, currency futures are not considered by many a bear market trading vehicle, even if your domestic currency is inflated. The leverage factor, plus the fact that all markets, including currency markets, are more volatile in bear times than in bull, make futures seem risky. But if you obey disciplines and use stop loss orders, they are useful. Yet, for the majority, it's easier to open a foreign bank account, with a time deposit, if you want to hedge your own currency, than to trade currencies in the futures market.

GLOBAL INVESTING IN MAJOR BEAR MARKETS

Terrorism will dampen global investing somewhat, but will not eliminate it. Even if terrorism did not exist, the natural tendency of most investors is to seek higher risk during a bull market than in a bear. Unless domestic inflation becomes a major issue, as it was during the 1970s in both the US and Europe, during a bear market, less people are willing to invest globally, either directly or via a mutual fund.

In addition, if a bear market bites hard, multinational companies will need to cut back. The first places they are likely to cut are the last places they invested in. It is likely that some multinationals will become less global in their reach over the next few years, for practical economic reasons. The international markets for new technology have, in the main, reached saturation point, even though there are, for example, billions of Chinese and Indians without computers. But high tech needs a basic infrastructure which many non-industrialized nations do not yet have. Until that infrastructure is created, there are, in many cases, not even the roads to truck the computers to consumers, let alone electrical outlets to plug them into.

A bear market is a time when companies regroup and consolidate rather than build new plants and try to nurture new business in foreign countries. And in this interconnected world, as America goes into a recession, most of the rest of the world follows.

In any future major bear market, with the exception of gold mining shares, there will probably be fewer foreign companies worth investing in, just as in the US.

As with multinational companies, a bear market is a time for the average investor to regroup and concentrate more on preserving capital, than taking risks in bull markets.

Part III
STRUCTURE OF BEAR MARKETS

"Many a healthy reaction has proved fatal."

Humphrey Neill

6
Secondary Reactions

In bear markets, we must turn our thinking upside down in many respects. For example, a "reaction" is now an up-move, because it is against the main trend.

Every leg-down in a bear market is interrupted by a secondary reaction, which may come in two or three phases.

These reactions are lifesavers for those who failed to take action when the bull market ended and are now stuck with giant losses. The secondary reaction gives us a chance to "bail out" at higher prices. It also gives an opportunity for shorting. Failure to sell out on this rally means you risk "taking a bath" when the next leg of the bear market comes into play at the end of the secondary reaction.

Of course, the possibility is ever present in any bear market that the rally will turn out to be a primary reversal. To distinguish between a true secondary and a primary reversal, I can probably do no better than to turn to the words of William Peter Hamilton, the successor of Charles Dow, who developed Dow's ideas into the Dow Theory we know today, and Robert Rhea, who further refined Dow Theory during the 1930s.

DECEPTIVE RALLIES

"An understanding of a secondary reaction," wrote Robert Rhea, "is needed by traders to about the same extent as a growing cotton crop requires sunshine." Yet, the secondary reaction is probably the most perplexing phenomenon with which the average investor must contend.

To begin with, let us define our terms. Readers are aware that a bull market leg swing is a broad upward movement of stocks, while a bull market reaction is an important decline against the primary trend. However, under Dow Theory, during a bear market, one must reverse the terminology. In bear markets, the primary legs are downward while the secondary reactions, or rallies, are upward movements against the prevailing primary trend.

Every bear market is made up of two or more downward legs (primary swings) and at least one secondary reaction. Some bear markets such as 1909–10 and 1987 were confined to the minimum. Others such as the bear markets of 1968 and 1973 had a number of primary legs and secondary reactions. The great 1929–32 affair was made up of no fewer than eight distinct primary legs and seven secondaries, a series not matched before or since.

"Secondary reactions," wrote Rhea, "are as necessary to the stock market as safety valves to steam boilers." In other words, when the stock market steam engine is straining and too many passengers have climbed aboard, the safety valve (secondary reaction) is released. Although many reasons are given for every move of this kind, it may be said that all secondaries serve the following purposes: (1) to correct a primary market movement that has gone too far in one direction, but where the underlying economic reasons for the primary direction have not changed enough to cause a reversal of the primary trend. (2) To dampen the speculative ardor of the amateur trader.

Despite their importance, most investors have great difficulty in recognizing the advent of a secondary reaction. "It may be conceded at once," wrote Hamilton, "that if it is hard to call the turn of a great bull or bear market, it is still harder to say when a secondary movement is due ..." To compound the hazards, secondaries often are mistaken for a true reversal of the primary trend. In bear markets, stockholders are anxiously awaiting the return of the bull tide; they are eager to seize upon any rally as the "turn."

In bull markets, most reactions end with a day or so of heavy volume, a characteristic that can be of real use in identifying the bottom. But a primary leg in a bear market may or may not end on heavy volume. Thus, the termination of a bear market leg and the beginning of a rally cannot always be spotted by volume indications alone.

It often happens, however, that, after an extended bear market decline, there will be a day or two of high volume. If the decline then continues *but volume shrinks drastically*, the odds favor an early reversal.

Moreover, while the precise turning point is difficult to recognize, after a long decline the price movement itself may give significant indications of an impending rally. These signs are described by Robert Rhea:

"A study of secondary reactions in bear markets will reveal that the
development of those movements is usually indicated by a series of
minor rallies and declines, with each rally generally carrying above
the preceding one and declines terminating above immediate
preceding lows. Such a formation in the averages forecasts a
secondary advance, even though the primary trend is down!"

It should be remembered, however, that both Transportations and Industrials
must confirm in such a movement before value inferences can be drawn.

Reactions (whether in bull or bear markets) nearly always consume *less* time
and are *more* violent than are movements in the direction of the primary trend.
It is not unusual for a 3-week rally in a bear market to retrace 30% to 60% of a
downward swing, which may have taken many months to complete.

"It is a tried rule which will help to guide us in studying the
secondary reaction movements that the change in the broad general
direction of the market is abrupt, while the resumption of the major
movement is appreciably slower."

Hamilton

Following a reaction in a bull market, a base is formed at or near the reaction
low, and it may take weeks or even months of accumulation before stocks
begin the next bull swing.

The explanation is simple: After a bull reaction, investors begin accumulat-
ing stocks and this is carried on as close to the lows as possible. But bear
market secondaries, in contrast, often present a bouncing or turn-on-a-dime
appearance; the rallies seem to spring from no visible base or area of support.
Again, the cause is evident. Bear market reactions invariably result from a
technical condition in which the market becomes oversold. The turn to the
upside may be set off by professional short sellers who realize the time has
come to cover.

Amateur short sellers, having made their move too late, quickly follow the
professionals' lead. Floor traders, sensing the reversal, throw the weight of
their buying behind the market. Thus, the rally is on. Obviously, such a
phenomenon is not a forecast of a fundamental turn but merely a technical
rebound in a market that has gone too far too fast.

It is invariably easier to call the end of a bear market rally than the
beginning. Rhea described one of the best methods for identifying the top:

"In such action the peak is frequently attained on a sudden increase
in activity lasting a few days. It is usually impossible to pick the turn
with any degree of precision; however if, after the high point has been
attained, a further rally shows a definite diminution in activity, it is
probable that an early resumption of the decline will occur."

Dullness following the peak of a bear market rally is a common danger sign. However, it is often confused by the average investor who fails to realize that the old adage, "Never sell a dull market," does not apply when the primary trend is down. Dow was the first to recognize the implications of dullness.

In 1902, he wrote, "... the action of the market after dullness depends chiefly upon whether a bull or bear market is in progress. In a bull market dullness is generally followed by advances, in a bear market by declines." He adds that, in bear markets, "... prices fall because values are falling, and dullness merely allows the fall in values to get ahead of the fall in prices."

Following a bear market rally, one Average often advances to a new high, but this may not be confirmed by the other Average. In such areas, dullness often occurs, after which both Averages sag below preceding decline points, and the primary downtrend is again resumed. Psychology during bear market rallies seems to follow a fairly consistent pattern.

"During secondary reactions in bear markets," wrote Rhea, "it is a fairly uniform experience for traders and market experts to become very bullish. They are usually bearish about the time the upturn comes."

The converse holds true of the psychology that precedes a bear market rally. Here, boardroom "oracles" are gloomy, investment services are pointing out the advantages of bonds and defensive stocks, and neophytes are trying their hand at shorting. The bad news, which already has been discounted in the downward swing, is appearing on all sides. At such times, a bear rally is in the making.

ACTING ON REACTIONS

Very long-term investors can ignore secondary reactions if they wish, but it's a difficult if not dangerous course and one fraught with sleeplessness. Mind you, the definition of a long-term investor in a bear market is one who holds short positions for the entire life of the bear.

I feel it's best to move in and out of the market *in conjunction with* secondary movements. Some of them retrace two-thirds (more or less) of the prior move, and this possibility is too large just to ride out.

And, of course, the short-term investor has no choice but to sell and buy in accordance with secondary moves. Thus, everyone needs to understand them and invest with them.

PSYCHOLOGY OF REACTIONS

In case I have not been clear enough on the rationale of a secondary reaction, let's point out that, after a collapse of prices, the market becomes temporarily oversold. And there remain a great mass of bulls who think any prices are bargain prices if they are substantially lower.

Also, there are those who went short at higher levels who now decide to take some profits. It is this combination that creates a major rally, or "secondary reaction" in bear markets.

The circumstances that bring the rally to an end are these: As prices rise to retrace about half the fall, traders will begin short selling again, and those who bought at the recent bottom will see nice profits, which they will begin to take. Those who have done nothing since the bear market started will see prices returning close to their cost price. Some begin to sell, willing to take a small loss in many cases. Since public confidence was shaken by the prior down-move, there will be few who will wait to see how far prices go; they will take a relatively reasonable price for their stock while they still can.

To round out a chapter on secondary reactions, I think readers will enjoy these words from Robert Rhea, who, during the big rally (or secondary reaction) in 1930, wrote:

> "I can remember having shorted stocks in early December 1929 after having completed a satisfactory short position in October. When the slow steady advance of January and February (1930) carried above previous intermediate highs, I became panicky and covered at considerable loss. With losses piling up every day, I forgot that the rally might normally be expected to retrace possibly 66% or more of the 1929 downswing. Nearly everyone was proclaiming a new bull market. Services were extremely bullish, and the upside volume was running higher than at the peak in 1929."

A STEP-BY-STEP ANALYSIS

It's always bullish just before the dawn—of a new downswing.

Another version of Rhea's conclusion can be found in the writings of market analyst Jim Sibbet. He wrote:

> "Whenever a sizable (over 10%) market movement occurs, it continues until the public, generally emotional, changes its mind and joins the movement. At first the tendency is toward disbelief, then gradually a few change, then more, and finally the overwhelming majority change their minds to such an extent that everyone will agree as to the prevailing majority opinion. When there is a conflict of opinion about the public's attitude, it is not overwhelming. The movement continues until there is no longer any doubt as to what the public's opinion is.

"The 1930 rally ran up until everyone was convinced another bull market had started. Right now there is considerable disagreement. Some think the public is still bearish and others think it has turned bullish, and still others think it is just beginning to turn bullish. Until there is unanimity of opinion, the current uptrends are likely to continue, because there are many people who are yet available to change their minds. Others who have already changed their minds are waiting for a good reaction to buy cheaper. This helps support the dips. It is the *process of changing* that makes prices move. After everyone's mind is made up, the movement stops and reverses."

THE SIZE OF REACTIONS

Perhaps the most important aspect of secondaries is their "average size." This is a facet few in the market today understand. Ask anyone you know how much a secondary reaction can be and they will likely reply: "one-third to two-thirds" of the ground lost.

This generalization can be very useful, but those who try to place an exact limit on secondary reactions are as doomed to failure as the weatherman who forecasts rainfall will be precisely one inch in the next 24 hours.

When a secondary goes beyond 66%, virtually everyone throws in the sponge, claiming loudly that the secondary is now a bull market. But history shows otherwise. A secondary can be as little as 10% and as much as 99.9%. As Robert Rhea defined it:

> "If we could say that the great majority of secondaries terminated around the 50% recovery point, speculation would be easy. Unfortunately, careful analysis shows that 7% of all reactions terminate after retracing 40–55%, 27% after retracing 55 to 70%, 8% after retracing 70 to 85%, with 14% of all secondary movements extending beyond 85% retracement."

Those percentages have probably not changed much in the 70 years since Rhea observed this.

SECONDARIES' PURPOSE

I wish I could remember where I read this, but I only recall that it was in the British Museum, when I was doing research for my first book on Bear Markets, nearly 40 years ago.

"To cure the exaggerations and extravagances of the preceding period of speculation is the function of a bear market. The difference between a technical reaction and a bear market is that the first is a purging of the *market*'s internal position, while the second is a thoroughgoing rectification of all excesses that have crept into the ensemble *economic structure*.

When contraction has proceeded far enough to remove the distortion and restore the balance, the bear market, from a fundamental standpoint, has ended."

It has fulfilled its function.

CONCLUSION

If you would be successful during bear markets, when those around you are losing their shirts, learn the signs of the secondary. Ignore those who declare that any observations about markets prior to 1980 are irrelevant to today's world. The people who say that are often the same types who, in the 1960s, were suspicious of anybody over 30 and, in the 1990s, claimed that the dot.coms were such a wonderful advance that the old rules of good business planning didn't apply any more. Scientists build on the wisdom of those who have gone before them. They would not dream of discarding the works of Newton or Galileo. Yet, the fashion today is to discard all stock market wisdom older than 10 years. You buy into this view at the peril of your portfolio and lifestyle.

7
Bear Market Legs

It's a bit easier to define legs (or phases) of bear markets than of bull markets because they are more compressed in time, more sharp in movement, more dramatic.

Yet, despite this, most people react to each secondary reaction as though it were the end of the bear market. My discussion of secondaries in the last chapter leaves one other aspect yet to be touched on in this area. I refer to bear market legs.

This is perhaps the most inexact aspect I have thus far discussed, so I shall not dwell long on it.

A leg is a phase of the market that can last anywhere from a few days to a few months, depending on how far you break it down.

A bear market can usually be broken into three legs or phases, and each of these in turn can be broken into three smaller legs, and each of those in turn into three. The major legs are rationalized as follows: the first major leg occurs when the euphoric expectations of unrealistically high stock prices are abandoned. The second leg occurs when more stocks are sold based on decreased economic conditions, decreased earnings, a rise in unemployment, etc. The third and final leg occurs when people cash out their stocks because their income has decreased so much that they simply need the money.

RECOGNIZING BEAR MARKET LEGS

Each leg in a bear market ends, almost without exception, on less volume than the volume occurring on the panic-declines or crashes.

For example, the crash in 1929 came on high volume very early in November, and the low of that bear leg came on considerably less volume in mid-November.

In 1937, the crash came on big volume in mid-October, but the low of the leg came on much less volume at the end of November.

In 1946, a pair of crashes, both on large volume, came in early May, and the leg's low came in early June on notably less activity.

In 1962, the market crashed on massive volume in the last week of May. But the low of the leg came at the end of June on much less volume.

In 1966, a similar pattern to 1962 was observed.

With the coming of the 1969 bear market, the pattern changed somewhat, probably because since 1969 the stock market has been more and more affected by political actions in addition to pure economic considerations. In all bear markets since, the decrease in volume, while noticeable, was far less pronounced than it had been in prior bear markets. In fact, the best way one was sure that the last bear leg had been seen was the sudden rise in volume while prices also rose.

Another reason for this distortion is that more and more money moving into the stock market is pension funds and thousands of new mutual funds. This means, when this money moves, it shows. The funds and institutions may not be right in their assessment of market conditions, but, at least temporarily, the sheer movement of such large amounts of money into any investment vehicle will cause that vehicle to rise. The vehicle having risen, traders, who jump on anything moving, will get aboard as well. This carries the move forward. In the last 5 years or so, as CNBC and other financial programs increasingly needed excitement to keep people watching, the tendency to *overdramatize* all news, both good and bad, goaded traders to buy or short those markets on a daily basis.

In the last 2 years, it has been fascinating to watch how many times the pre-market futures prices and direction was the opposite to how the market eventually finished the day, as traders made bets against the trend which they were pretty certain would occur once the market opened and "normal folks" bought and sold.

We saw this particularly in the 2 weeks following the reopening of Wall Street after the September 11 attack, when the Dow and the Nasdaq dropped like stones. Yet, markets quickly returned to levels that existed before the attack, once traders covered their shorts and went back to the serious business of making markets.

A concept sometimes heard is that, of three legs, the first is down (in a bear market), the second up, the third down. But a more widely accepted version is that the three legs are all down in a bear market or up in a bull.

Statistically, it has been pretty well proven that major bear markets all have a minimum of two legs and potentially from three to eight.

The crash of 1929 had, so far, the greatest number of legs of all bear markets in history: eight. A repeat performance is not out of the question, but in my opinion, extremely unlikely—in any future major bear market.

Legs are simply a way of keeping track of the market on a broader perspective scale. Thus, when a market moves in a new direction and then seems to grind to a halt, amid talk that "it's all over," you can shake your head and figure there is bound to be at least another leg in the same direction shortly. The perspective of market legs gives your thinking balance, just as your body's legs give your body balance.

TECHNICAL RATIONALE BEHIND LEGS

The technical rationale for legs is that the market moves in waves or series. When enough momentum has accumulated to push the market, let's say down radically, there surely must be enough pressure to cause it to follow through, to continue to press on despite setbacks, in a *series* of waves.

It would be quite illogical to see a market drop sharply from high ground and then recover and zoom on immediately to new highs again. Like a runner whose pace has been broken by a fall, he has to get in stride all over again, and this takes time—for momentum, speed, and direction.

Tidal waves usually have follow-up waves in the same manner—sometimes smaller, sometimes bigger than the first.

The Elliott Wave Theory, which attempts to predict the market almost entirely on this wave principle, maintains that, in the stock market, these waves come in a series of five, and, until five have been completed, it is unlikely for a major change of trend. But regardless of number, the principle of multiple waves or phases or legs is more or less scientific.

"LEGS" ILLUSTRATED

Figure 7.1 illustrates "legs" or waves or steps. We see three clearly defined legs. From A to B is the first leg, from B to C the recovery. From C to D the second leg, from D to E the recovery. From E to F the third leg. (If you prefer to think in broader movements, you can eliminate the second leg and call the move from C to F a single leg, which is technically more correct.) We then note the recovery movement. From F to G, the first leg up; with G to H the reaction.

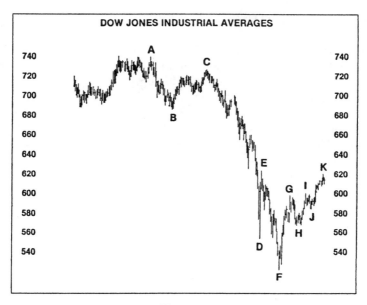

Figure 7.1

From H to I, the second leg up; with I to J the reaction. From J to K (as far as this figure takes us) is an unfinished third leg.

By studying legs, one gets a better idea of where you are and what may lie ahead. For example, an investor watching this chart would have noticed that when peak C was past, it was very likely that another leg down was due. Then, when the market dropped below the level of point B, a down leg was a virtual certainty. Selling out at that time, though well below the top, was still well above the lows. And short positions at that moment would have paid off handsomely.

NOTHING IS CERTAIN

Because nothing is certain in the market, you must always assume it's possible for a reversal to take place. Thereafter, even after only a single bear leg down, you should start watching (à la 1987). After two bear legs, you should be much more alert, and after three legs, you can begin to anticipate a reversal with growing conviction.

Of course, the same principle holds true in reverse in bull markets. But, somehow, people in the market find it hard to turn their thinking upside down to apply normal rules in reverse during bear markets.

WATCH RELATIVE LEVELS

Remember to watch for a rally high closing above a prior rally high, then dipping, but holding below the former low. When you see this in a bear market, it's time to assume the new trend is up.

This premise works in determining when a bear market is starting. Thus, when prices fall lower than the last decline and then rise but fail to reach the last rally high, you must take the position that a downtrend is under way. And all trends must then be assumed to remain in effect until reversed again. This can be a matter of days, weeks, months, or even years.

Part IV
TOOLS FOR MEASURING BEAR MARKETS

"I have always thought, that if . . . even in the very presence of dizzily spiraling [stock] prices, we had all continuously repeated, 'two and two still make four,' much of the evil might have been averted. Similarly, even in the general moment of gloom in which this foreword is written, when many begin to wonder if declines will never halt, the appropriate abracadabra may be: 'They always did.'"

Bernard Baruch in July 1932, the month of the absolute bottom of the 1929 crash. Quoted by Andrew Tobias in his Foreword to *Extraordinary Popular Delusions and the Madness of Crowds*, by Charles Mackay, Three Rivers Press, 1980

8
Tools to Help You Recognize and Survive a Bear Market

"We have more ability than will power, and it is often an excuse to ourselves that we imagine that things are impossible."

Rochefoucauld, 1665

It's not necessary to debate the merits of the "fundamental approach" versus the "technical approach" to justify this chapter. If you like to judge stocks on the basis of fundamentals (earnings, cash flow, book value, corporate officer changes, news of new products, estimates of future earnings, and so forth), that's fine.

It does not detract from the technical approach, which generally can paint a bigger and more time-related picture. Many people use both.

THE FUNDAMENTAL APPROACH

But, if you rely only on fundamentals, you *never* know whether you have all the necessary facts to make an informed judgment. Some are purposely hidden, withheld, or delayed. Others just may not come to your attention. You have to read everything in sight to make sure that you are not missing a "revised estimate of earnings," or a news story about the death of the board chairman, or a new government contract, or news about the order backlog or a contract cancellation.

And if you use the Internet for research, false rumors are intentionally circulated to enable criminals to capitalize on the reaction to rumors.

THE TECHNICAL APPROACH

The beauty of technical analysis is that it is "scam proof." It relies on your ability to read the charts and the price data, not on public or insider information.

With the technical approach, you know that what you know about a specific index reading is all there is to know. There is no more. Nobody can con you and you can be sure nothing has gotten by you. The price is the price. Follow the money.

There may be many ways to *interpret* each index figure, and new technical indexes and measurements are ever being devised, but the fact remains that once you look at, for example, the low-price-stock-index figure for this week, you know all there is to know, statistically, in that area. There is a satisfaction and mental peace in this knowledge, not to mention a safety factor.

In this chapter, I deal only with that part of the technical approach involved with tools, which means methods of measurement of various things in the stock market deemed worth measuring.

New tools are being fashioned every month in an attempt to make more of a science of the art of investing. And computer buffs delight in finding ever more sets of numbers to crunch. But my best advice is to use a number of tried and true tools. Examine each new one as it comes along. If a new one appears to add something to the mental picture your existing tools provide, add it to your toolbox. But stay with several tools you get to know, like your family, year after year. That way you come to have a "feel" for the way each one handles in every kind of market.

KNOW YOUR TOOLS INTIMATELY

It's usually better to know a tool well—even though you may surmise it's not the best tool available—than to use a great many tools that time prevents you from getting to know one tool like a friend. It's like an artist with an old brush. He knows there are better, newer brushes, but he knows what he can do with the old one. He knows its idiosyncrasies. And every tool has those!

Some people believe that a minimum of market tools is desirable, like two or three. Or even one. But the danger here is acute. If you only rely on one like, say, the Mutual Fund Cash/Assets Ratio, you will eventually learn to your sorrow that there are times when this (or any) tool just doesn't work.

Even the use of two or three tools doesn't set things right, because often tools are "silent" and fail to say anything, and if you have silent tools and one is giving a false clue, you are better off with none.

Thus, it's best to use as many indicators, or tools, as you can handle. But make sure you really understand them; to have so many tools that you have no time to review and develop them lowers their overall value.

YOUR OWN PERSONAL INDEX OF MARKET ACTION

By putting all your indicators and tools together and having each one "vote" each week with a weighted vote (based on the past performance of each), you'll get a big view of the market.

Weighting the indexes is a tricky job, both time-consuming and difficult of appraisal. Yet, it must be done. You may find a better approach than I use, but here's my method: Study an indicator over as long a period as possible. Note how dependable it was in previous bull or bear swings. Calculate what percent of the time it was right. Thus, if it was 85% accurate, it could be given a weight or vote, of say four points on any future occasion when it gives a similar cue to those of the past. If it has a current reading only approaching a normal cue level, you may decide to "vote" it this week with a weight of only two points.

Also, it's probably best to "vote" your indicators in two ways: (1) the actual number of indexes voting plus or minus, and (2) the total points (or votes) cast by the indexes, according to the weights you have assigned them.

When points and number of indexes are both positive or negative—and by a safe margin—then market direction is clear. If they conflict or are nearly even, the safe course is to wait.

Also, you can vote each index by time category—short term, medium, and long. Set up your own premise for how long is short term (to you), and so forth. It makes no difference how long it is, so long as you understand it and interpret everything by those standards.

Just how good your composite index will be is up to you. You will have your own versions, concepts, preferences, and experiences. It would probably be impossible to give a formula for a total personal index even if we had a full book just for that. So, in the limited space I have, I can only skeletonize.

But, however simple you make your personal index, you will still be ahead of the millions of investors who got into the market during the latter part of the 1990s with little or no idea of how to measure market strength or weakness and who have substantial losses, but who have no tools to tell them whether to grimly hold on for the next bull market, or to sell out on the next rally. You'll be miles ahead of those poor souls whose only guide is the TV talking heads.

BASIC TOOLS

Let's deal with a few relatively dependable indicators, or tools. Mind you, these fellows shouldn't be allowed to think for you. They could lead you into a trap, particularly if you obtain them via an online service that calculates them for you. The point of any market tool is to add grist for the mill, to supplement that inner judgment we call gut feel or intuition—a pre-verbal wisdom we are all born with, but often has been educated out of us by the time we are adults. Tools should be used as guides. Your thinking should generally conform to them, but only within their broad guidelines. And, as you gain experience with your tools, you will learn when to listen to them and when to ignore some of them.

The stock market is probably the toughest field in the world because the keenest minds are in it, in competition with you. Thus, how you use your tools or weapons may well determine how you fare. Note: a number of the indicators listed here can be obtained on a daily basis from various online services, thus saving you, the investor, the job of having to calculate them yourself:

1. Advance–decline line. By subtracting the daily number of advances from declines (or declines from advances) and subtracting (or adding) that difference from a running cumulative total (from an arbitrary starting figure), you measure what the great mass of the market is doing. This is surely the most basic and important tool of them all. What it reflects is usually more significant than what the market averages are saying. Observe the way in which it diverges from the averages for the best clues. Also: note that it "meets resistance" (or support), usually, in the same way individual stocks do, at places in the past where it stalled.

2. New highs–new lows. Total the last 5 days of the daily new highs; divide by five. That's the 5-day moving average. Do the same for the lows. Chart the highs in black, the lows in red. Observe whether the highs remain on top during a reaction that has interrupted a major upswing. (If not, it's usually fatal to the upswing.) And vice versa. Note whether each successive peak of highs or lows is higher than the previous one as a guide to the soundness of the primary trend. Also, compare highs with highs, lows with lows.

You may wonder why I recommend a 5-day moving average here and a 10-day in other places. While these findings are not foolproof, nonetheless the best conclusions, thus far reached, show that in the case of the hi–low index, for example, fewer than 5 days make a moving average too erratic. Such an average bounces all over the chart, making it hard to find any pattern or trend line. Conversely, more than five days smooths it out so much that it can hardly be seen to move, and you can't get much of a message from it. Thus, it seemed 5 days was best for most purposes.

But, there are no laws in this field. You can create and mold and alter to suit yourself.

Also, the size of your moving average may depend on whether you are a daily trader, a short-term trader, a medium-term investor, a long-term holder, or some of each. The longer term you are, the broader time period you will usually want to measure.

3.   Odd-lot balance index (odd lotters buy less than 100 shares). Divide the daily odd-lot purchases total into the daily odd-lot sales. Totals above 100% show the small investor selling more shares than he buys. Below 100%, readings reflect on-balance buying on the part of this so-called bad-timing investor. The only readings of significance are the changes of percent, not the switch from sell to buy or buy to sell. A move from 70 to 90% is as important as from 95% to 115%. Pros often sell when the small investor suddenly buys, or buy when the odd lotter suddenly sells. But the odd-lot is only significant when held up as a mirror to the market trend. And you should act only when the odd lotters depart from their norm. They usually buy in the early stages of declines and sell in rising markets.

4.   Odd-lot trading ratio. Add daily odd-lot sales and purchases together. Divide that figure by total market volume for the day. Then, cut your answer in half, because market volume represents a sale and a purchase together as one unit, while odd-lot figures take them separately. The result is a figure between 7 and 13%. 10% is normal. Below that is bullish. Above 10% is bearish.

5.   Odd-lot short sales index. When the odd lotters are shorting on a big scale, it's about time the market turned up. When they are shorting very little, a decline is not necessarily imminent, but the ground is fertile for it. This index should be kept daily, and as a 10-day moving average, where it is most accurate. The number of odd-lot short sales is available each day in the press. A falling line accompanies rallies; a rising line accompanies declines. Thus, you can ride the trend as long as it lasts, then get off quickly.

A very alert student of this index should also watch for special arbitrage transactions that could affect this ratio.

6.   Volume. There are probably 25 different ways to measure volume, and there is probably nothing more important to measure and understand.

JOSEPH GRANVILLE ON VOLUME

In his book, *A Strategy of Daily Stock Market Timing for Maximum Profit*, he says:

"The first series of declines in a bear market may be accomplished on light volume and this must be bearishly interpreted simply because the quality of leadership will be excellent on the downside. Volume will be light on the early stage of the decline because the public believes that the decline is nothing more than one of the usual previous dips in a bull market and the result they expect will be another buying opportunity. The early selling is therefore done by the professionals. When the decline does not stop, the public becomes concerned and starts to sell stocks and the volume gradually rises on the accelerating decline.

"As the decline becomes more rapid, the public gets more and more frightened and now stocks are being dumped. This sends the volume still higher and a 'selling climax' results.

"Recognizing this climax as a sign for a technical rebound, the professionals now start buying and the market goes into a technical rebound.

"If the fundamental business background is showing some signs of weakening at this juncture, then such a rebound in the market would probably be considered as a selling opportunity, further declines are yet to come. This pattern can be summarized as: First phase of decline on light volume—professionals are selling, and public remains confident. Second phase of decline on heavier volume—professionals are selling, and public disbelief over the decline causes them to lighten up. Third phase of decline on still heavier volume leading to a selling climax—professionals finish their selling, and public confidence, now shaken, brings in a deluge of stocks. Fourth phase of decline—temporary technical rebound on professional short covering and general professional buying while public continues to sell.

"The point here is to stress the fact that the most serious declines in stock market history usually started with what looked like a series of meaningless light volume declines; at least the public thought they were meaningless. The quality of leadership was the key."

You may create a method of measuring volume that is better than those in frequent use. Personally, I feel improved volume-measuring indexes are badly needed. Volume, in my opinion, is both the most important, least understood, and worst-measured factor in the stock market.

Charting pure daily market volume is essential. One can also chart volume hourly, weekly, or monthly, and a 10-day moving average is important too. Then, you can chart the volume of the DJIA or S&P only or any of the other averages or combination of any of them. The variables are almost endless and each has its own special set of interpretive rules, most of which you can learn from simply watching volume figures. Some advisory services regularly comment on these as well as other sources, so one is always exposed to various interpretations. Price tends to follow volume, as a loose rule of thumb.

DOW ON VOLUME

In May 1901, Charles Dow wrote:

> "Great activity means great movement whenever the normal balance between buyers and sellers is violently disturbed."

In January of that year, he wrote:

> "Dullness usually runs to advance in a bull market and into decline in a bear market."

GARTLEY ON VOLUME

H.M. Gartley was a great technician in the 1930s. He did more work on volume than any other man. In 1933, he wrote:

> "Note that bear market cycles begin on reduced volume. As the major (downward) phase develops, volume increases and this phase ends in a selling climax on heavy volume. The ensuing rally (corrective phase) is accompanied by declining volume, which dwindles until the rally loses momentum completely, and the major trend is resumed in a new bear cycle. . . . Bear market rallies start out of active selling climaxes."

Note that the first six bear market rallies, following the 1929 top, came out of heavy trading. But the rally in July 1932 came out of extreme dullness, indicative of a major reversal (a new bull market began on July 8, 1932). The rationale behind the diminishing volume in bear markets is simply that the public loses interest as it loses money. Also, they have less capital to trade with, owing to those losses.

7.   DJIA 30-week moving average. Add the last 30 Friday closing prices of the Dow Jones Industrials (as with any average) and divide by 30. Then, each week, add the new DJIA figure and subtract the 31st week back. Chart it alongside the DJIA. Alternatively, this can be done via computer chart services automatically. But doing it manually, or at least knowing how, gives you a feel for the process. Generally, the 30-week moving average (of a stock or an average) stays above the current price in bear markets, below it in bull markets. It gives cues and clues when the price attempts to penetrate the moving average. If penetration lasts for several weeks, it can usually be regarded as a valid signal. Some prefer a 40-week moving average. It is probably best to keep both if you have the time. Also, a 10-week moving average is believed to be highly

sensitive and useful for short-term trading. You can create your own moving average as an experiment.

8. Overbought–oversold index. There are many forms for this index and the best one has yet to be invented. Quite popular is the 10-day moving average of the difference between advances and declines. When a rally moves up too fast, the advances pile up and an overbought condition is created, which "usually" is soon corrected. The same in reverse, with declines. About +1,200 is considered overbought land, and −1,600 is the start of oversold territory. When this (or any other) indicator goes wrong, however, it can cause you heavy losses if you rely too heavily on just this one. You always tell yourself: "I'm too smart to ever rely on any one index," but when the time comes and you see an extreme reading on some usually reliable indicator, you often get carried away in the desire to get a jump on the crowd with this apparent solid backing.

I have a personal method of interpreting the overbought–oversold 10-day index, which is even more useful than the traditional approach just outlined. If you chart this back for some months, you will see how you can apply normal stock chart analysis and get better results. You'll find rare wedges appear, and longer-term (multi-month) trend lines are fabulously successful as cues when broken up or downside. As this is a smoothed-out (10-day) version of what the market is really doing (advances–declines), it's logical that critical information is hidden here awaiting your discovery. Also, note that some stocks/commodities are more responsive to this (or any tool) than others. If you track their history, you'll find such varying sensitivity of great help.

9. Confidence index. No market book is complete without a comment on Barron's Confidence Index. This figure represents the ratio between the yield on high-risk and low-risk bonds and supposedly shows the thinking of the elite money minds. The record of the CI has been distorted by many to force its record into proving it is always right. I have made a 5-week and a 10-week moving average of it and also charted it raw over many years and cannot escape the conclusion that when it works, it works; and when it doesn't, it doesn't. It's batting average some years is 100%. In other years: zero. It's just *one* tool in your tool kit.

10. Short interest. This is published between the 15th and the 20th of each month. The amount of shares sold short has a relationship to the future since those shares must be bought back someday. This must be used in conjunction with the Short Interest Ratio.

Arbitrage disfigures short interest. Arbitrage is an aspect of short interest that again points out the danger of blindly reading a big short interest as bullish, or a small one as bearish.

Often, a stock will be shorted as a means of taking a small profit in a special situation via an arbitrage action. And, in the last several years, online advisory services have sprung up where arbitrage is a major investment strategy. Several circumstances can cause arbitrage trading, and it does not mean people are actually shorting because they are bearish. It is a process where traders buy and sell the same stock, often holding both long and short until the proper time. This can come about, for example, in a planned takeover of one company by another.

Arbitrage is a term applied to transactions where a trader may buy the convertible bonds of a company and sell the stock into which the bonds may be converted. The bonds, after conversion, furnish cover for the sale of the stock. Arbitrage is also used to take advantage of the different pricing for the same item between, say, New York and London, or Frankfurt and Hong Kong.

I am discussing arbitrage here primarily as a *distorter* of short interest. So, bear in mind that it can, at times, easily amount to 5–10% or more of the market's short total. In many instances, the total short interest monthly direction is contrary to truth "if" you subtract the arbitrage shorts.

11. The Short Interest Ratio. This measures the market volume against the shorts, once a month. Short interest is simply divided by current average daily volume. When the ratio is large (2% or higher), it's bullish, for it means there are too many shorts for the amount of volume going on. When it's small (1% and below), it's bearish.

There are refinements you can make. Maybe a 5-day moving average of volume could be computed and a new ratio calculated weekly from that.

12. Brokers' Free Credit Balance Index. The amount of money (credit) held in customer's accounts is latent buying power. Measuring this amount monthly is of more than passing interest. It tells us, rather reliably, what stage of a bull or bear market we are in. Customers tend to use up more of this credit cash as a bull market is reaching its top. They tend to let more of this money stand idle during the first half of a bull run because they aren't convinced yet. These figures are found in Barron's, as are most statistics you need for most indexes. Barron's and a quality daily newspaper with good financial coverage, and an online statistical service are musts for keeping up your indicators. And though, these days, it is possible to obtain many of the indicators, mentioned here, ready made over the Internet, until you are familiar with them, I strongly advise you to physically plot them yourself to get a feel for each one—and the market.

Just as the best way to learn new computer software is to use it, and merely being told how it works doesn't give you an understanding of how it handles, so it is with market indicators. Plot them by hand until you reach a point where they become part of your inner "pre-verbal" wisdom and judgment.

Once you reach a point when you can sense what the latest numbers mean for the overall market picture, even before you have entered them on your charts, then are you ready to have somebody else (a computer program or service) do the plotting for you.

13.   Debit Balances Index. This is the mirror image of the above index. Information here represents the money owed to brokers in margin accounts; thus, it is the reverse of the Credit Balance Index. This index represents shrewder traders. Thus, this total tends to rise during the first two stages of bull markets. It generally tops out in the last portion of a bull market and drops steadily through the bear market following.

14.   Nasdaq indexes. The Nasdaq reflects the more speculative aspects of Wall Street, and no bull market can long exist unless or until the speculative element is active. Blue chips alone never made a bull market. You should make an advance–decline line for the Nasdaq the same way as you do for the DJIA. Also, a highs–lows index can be made. Volume can be plotted. Watch for disparity between the Nasdaq and the DJIA or S&P. The Dow can't make and sustain a bull market by itself, and the Nasdaq is likely to top out and go into a sustained decline before the Dow Industrials, as happened during 2000. And any rally in the Dow will not herald a major new bull market, unless the move is reflected in the Nasdaq.

15.   Resistance Index. This has various styles and forms. An easy method is as follows: If the market is up (as measured by the DJIA), subtract the advances (total issues advancing) from the issues traded. Then, divide the figure by the total issues traded. If the market is down, do the same thing using the declines instead of the advances. This percentage shows the level of resistance to whatever the market is doing.

This calculation can be made on a weekly or daily basis. Unless you are a day trader, the daily will serve no purpose for you. In the weekly form (using figures for the week as a whole and ignoring daily figures), it usually shows resistance between 30% and 60%. Normally, it stays well within the middle zone of those two extremes, but, when it leaps up or falls down to touch those levels, it is showing strong resistance.

16.   Leadership Index. The average *price* of the daily volume leaders shows the *kind* of leadership the market is enjoying. If this tends to fall on upswings or rise on downswings, it's bearish. I like this indicator and hardly anyone follows it anymore, which makes it work better.

17.   Percent of advances index. Divide the daily advances by the issues

traded. This is another way of approaching the overbought–oversold problem. A 10-day moving average is probably best. In charting it, you'll discover how to interpret it, for the extremes become obvious cues. When it falls below 40%, it's a signal of weakness ahead.

18. Gold Shares Index. This (as with most indices) can be kept daily or weekly, or both. If you are an active investor or trader, you need this on a daily basis. There are several Gold indices. The Gold-Bug index (my favorite), the Toronto gold index, the *Financial Times* gold index, and the South African gold index. Or you can create your own by posting the prices of at least six gold shares into a composite index. Compare the net change each time with the net change of the Dow Jones Industrials. If they both rise together, it's bearish, especially if the gold's net change is large. Also, when the gold index has a large net change and the DJIA moves in the opposite direction or moves down, the action is predicting the market will continue in the same direction the next day.

SOME PERSONAL FAVORITE INDICES

1. DJIA 10-day moving average of internal volume. Don't tackle this one unless you like work. Here, you total the volume of all the Dow stocks that rose, and those that fell, separately. Make a 10-day moving average of the plus-volume and also of the minus-volume. Subtract these totals daily, and chart the differential as a plus or minus figure. Through the use of trend lines, this chart will show you blue-chip strength. Breaking a trend line is usually a valid signal. Other cues can come from normal chart formations.

2. DJIA resistance. Similar to above, but limited only to those DJIA stocks that were unchanged. This volume is posted on a daily basis only, not a 10-day moving average. On days when the unchanged volume is high, it is usually a fairly safe assumption that whatever the market did that day is "wrong" and will be reversed the next day.

3. DJIA volume ratio. Get the volume of all DJIA stocks. Divide that figure by the volume for the market as a whole. This percentage ratio represents what share the blue chips have of the market total. No "canned explanation" here will do, as experimentation brings the best result. But, loosely, a high ratio is usually bullish, a low ratio bearish, read against the market background. The range is about 8 to 14%.

4. Advance–decline 200-day line. Same principle as 200-day line for the DJIA or any stock, but its significance is often greater. The principle of 200 days is that this covers a long enough period so as to be representative of short, medium, and long-term investors' thinking. A 1-year

view is taken by a large number of people for tax reasons, and an index spanning this period thereby gains significance.

5.   Nasdaq volume leaders. Record the plus and minus action of the top five Nasdaq most active stocks. You can chart it on a daily basis, or a 3, 5, 6, or 7-day moving average basis, or weekly. I tend to interpret this one very loosely as giving a bullish signal on the first day (in many weeks) that it records five consecutive pluses and a bear market signal on the first five minuses. You can use this formula for the S&P and DJIA also.

In general, I do not use indexes based on the Russell, or Wilshire, because these are not averages most investors watch. They are not the ones CNBC gets excited about. Though they give you a fuller picture of what the overall market is doing, their movements do not psychologically move investors to act.

STOCK MARKET NOT A THING APART

To many, perhaps most investors, the stock market is treated as a thing apart from life, not a reflection of our total world. Somehow, people believe it is perfectly logical for the stock market to rise while the business climate becomes antagonistic and/or riskier. Even in today's supposedly global, interdependent world, very few people consider happenings in other countries when buying American shares. But communications are so immediate that what happens in Tokyo or Brussels has a direct bearing on the stocks the guy in Kansas or Kentucky is considering buying or selling.

It is only within a broad international economic/political/cultural context that you can successfully use your market tools. A knowledge of global economics, global politics, and global cultural considerations have become vital market tools. You should listen to daily international newscasts, and read at least one foreign daily newspaper. If you can read a foreign language newspaper, so much the better, but, if not, then the *International Herald Tribune*, or the *Financial Times* of London are prime choices. All foreign media give a global perspective in ways the US press never does! Unlike the US, most countries with credible stock markets are too small and vulnerable to live in the sort of insulated bubble of non-awareness that America has inhabited for most of its history.

Only time will tell if the events of September 11, 2001 will cause the American media to produce more thoughtful, balanced and non-provincial news, of the sort the *Financial Times* or the nightly BBC News produces. But, as of this writing, there are few signs that anything has changed much. Provincialism still rules.

VALUES AT BEAR MARKET BOTTOMS

Too little has been said about values at bear market bottoms and at other turning points. It is one of our safest, if not best indicators. It refers to the percent of dividend yield of the DJIA stocks, and, as such, is a measuring rod for what kind of return or value you get for a dollar invested. At the September 1929 peak, the DJIA average yield was 3.3%. At the crash low, 2 months later, the yield was 5.2%.

During the 1929–32 (and the great majority of *all* bear markets), higher yields came about through falling stock prices. The yields went from 3.3% to 10.3%.

You can't know when yields are too high, or too low. But, if you are constantly aware of whether yields are "relatively high" (or low), you will keep your mind in a constant state of alert, so that stock action will fit into perspective and won't surprise you. It is often the surprise-shock that stuns investors and renders them incapable of making rational decisions when it counts most. A prepared mind is not caught off guard.

TWO WARNINGS

1. If an indicator points to the market going up next, for example, don't assume it must be boxed into a period of precisely one full, precise market day. The market may rise sharply for the first 3 hours of the next day, then fall to the floor. The indicator was right as far as it could see within its limits. Ditto on a weekly basis. You'll learn these limits for *each* index with experience. Watch *what* happens regardless of time. Think in terms of *points*, not hours, weeks, or months.

2. Don't rely on indicators to work mechanically. Try to get the "feel" of the situation. It's not easy to come by. But, to whatever degree, however slight, you can attain that feeling, it's worth the effort. It comes easy to some, hard to others, like learning languages. And this *is* a language—the language of Wall Street. Learning to see or feel the relationships of the indicators or to sense the background against which they are "talking" at any given moment is the art of *real* stock market analysis.

The seeds of every decline are planted during the late stages of every upturn, and it follows that the promise of a new uptrend comes into being during a decline. It's part of the job of your tools, or indicators, to detect these seeds.

YOU CANNOT IGNORE INDICATORS

It's a mistake to think you are too lazy or busy to bother with indicators, for in truth we are all index-conscious all the time in ways of which we are only vaguely aware. You are bound, for example, to be interested in at least a few from among those that pass before you automatically: Federal Reserve action such as interest rate cuts, figures on production, consumer confidence, cost of living index, or the percent of unemployed. Or your brokerage service provides indexes for you as a customer. Or the advisory service you get is keen on Bank Credit statistics or odd lots.

You can't escape indicators. So this is my recommendation: If you can't fight 'em, join 'em. Instead of having statistics tossed at you randomly, often selectively by the media to build a case for their particular point of view, take control. Put them in some order to get perspective. Keep your own indicators so that when figures pop up in the press or conversation, you can fit them into an ongoing long-term pattern.

Virtually all indicators have value. It's up to you to determine which ones best talk to you. And you may create new ones or variations of old ones that may be more effective than those in use today. And you'll learn to weigh them on the basis of their degree of success in the past.

Use as many as you can possibly spare time for. The greater the span of your indicators, the greater your understanding. Knowledge is power, now and ever more.

AUTHOR'S WARNING

One very important final and cautionary word belongs in this chapter. There is nothing wrong with indexes, but there is often a lot wrong with the interpretations some people make from them. So, if you read an advisory service or hear a broker say that such and such an index is now bearish—don't believe it until you have checked it out yourself, on your own charts. That is, unless you have found from experience that this brokerage or that service knows that index well enough, that you are satisfied they are interpreting it correctly.

Also, unless you analyze them yourself, you don't know if their interpretation is short, medium, or long term.

KEY TO TECHNICAL SUCCESS

The single most important key or guide to remember, in my opinion, in this area of using technical tools for buy-and-sell cues is this: The success of the technical approach can be realized only when the indicators are heavily weighted in your favor.

Let me paraphrase that for emphasis. In working with indicators you have carefully been plotting for months, it is tempting to lean on them heavily and to act on their readings when you have, let's say, 6 saying buy, 3 saying sell, and 21 standing neutral. But, unless you have a truly heavy weight on the side of buy or sell (like 17 buy, 4 sell, 9 neutral—depending on which indicators you use and how you weight them), you cannot hope to succeed, on average.

The same rule applies to individual stocks. Unless you can see at least the potentiality of a stock moving up 30 to 60% or more, it is not normally worth buying (except for scalp trading). Yet, people who know this and follow it in stocks will ignore the principle in their indicators.

TOO MANY TECHNICIANS?

Is there a danger that there can be too many technicians in the market? I doubt it. Provided you do your own analysis and don't just rely on some technical computer program that creates buy and sell signals based on their software, you will stay ahead of the crowd no matter how many other people use technical analysis.

Technicians have "an influence" on stock action, and they provide leadership to a lot of non-technicians out of all proportion to their number, but they are not of themselves a big group. It's too much work (being a technician) for it ever to rise above the 10% level. And the number of really first-class, well-rounded, experienced technical–chartist–analysts with a moderately decent record of right guesses over wrong and the ability to express themselves is probably only a few hundred, in a world of millions of investors.

9
Tools that "Change Shape" in Bear Markets

Stock market tools don't act the same, necessarily, in good weather and bad, rather like your grandfather's bad back or trick wrist/knee. When it's raining on Wall Street, some market indicators must be looked at differently.

Your car acts differently in freezing weather and so do many indicators in bear markets. Most people's actions are different in bright sunshine from their behavior in dreary, cold, overcast climes. Some market indicators are the same. Bull markets are akin to bright weather, when most wheels run without a hitch.

OVERBOUGHT–OVERSOLD INDEX

An example is the overbought–oversold index, which, in a bull market, reaches a certain level and says, "Stop, now we turn about for awhile." In a bear market, the oversold end of the teeter-totter can go out into the wild blue yonder *without* meaning very much. Even so, it too has a vague limit, a measurable limit area. But, unless you are aware that the rules have changed in a bear market, you'll think a turn is due too soon.

If you study the past history of your pet indices in bear markets, you'll see whether or not they perform a bit differently.

CONFIDENCE INDEX

Barron's Confidence Index is another example. It often performs very differently in bear markets than in bull; the time lag changes.

VOLUME

One also interprets volume differently in a bear market, which is probably the most important single measuring rod in the entire marketplace. (See Chapter 8 for more on volume in bear markets.)

It is probably no understatement to say 98% of market investors have no concept of bear market volume patterns. They go on in blissful ignorance using bull market formulas for volume.

MONTHLY SHORT INTEREST

Another interesting example is the monthly short interest. Almost everyone sees this as a big support under the market. In bull markets, this is true. But, in bear markets, a large portion of short interest is "invested" with the (down) trend. Those who are short are in *no hurry* to cover. Some will remain short for years, if necessary, until they feel a new bull market is genuinely under way. Thus, an amateur can be misled into buying when short interest climbs to its first new high in a bear market. It's premature.

You will learn much of the difference between the reactions of your favorite indicators in bull and bear markets by studying them in both bull and bear years.

ODD-LOT SHORT SELLING

You'll find that daily odd-lot short selling figures at say 400,000 are, in a bull year, regarded as extremely high, but in a bear year are regarded as relatively low.

DAILY NEW HIGHS AND LOWS

In bear markets, one watches the daily new highs and lows differently. If the highs can remain superior on a new down leg in a bear market, there is a chance you are seeing a reversal, from bear to bull.

DJIA 200-DAY LINE

The DJIA 200-day line is regarded quite differently in bear markets. Although the principles are the same, unless you are conscious of the new market atmosphere that prevails when you go from bull to bear, your interpretations can be quite wrong for some time.

BETTER TO DO IT YOURSELF

This is not a book on indicators alone, and I cannot spell out how every indicator works in *every* respect, let alone how each works in bull markets as distinct from bear. Furthermore, it is more beneficial to readers not to have things spelled out in detail, for then they tend to follow such outlines as though they were "the law." It's better to think out the *rationale* of everything in the stock market yourself. Then, not only do you understand the market better and know the whys, but you also know its limitations, and your thinking process has been sharpened in the process.

In closing this section, let me liken the sense of it to fashion. You will still be wearing clothes next year but the style will be different. Likewise, you will still be watching indicators in bear markets but the interpretation will be different.

ROBERT RHEA'S FORECASTS

More light about identifying the end of bear markets can be brought to the fore by quoting Robert Rhea again. One month before the final bottom in 1938, he wrote:

> "In the opinion of this writer we are emerging from the second phase and going into the third and *final portion* of the bear market. This may last for a week, a month, or many months."

On what did he base this perfect forecast? Stocks at that time had lost major portions of their value, the DJIA had dropped, and, in March, the yield on the 30 Industrials was 7.3%. The time was ripe on the basis of fundamentals and values for the birth of a new bull market.

In contrast to the 1938 situation, the "bull market signal" of 1930 was obviously suspect. Nevertheless, it caught Rhea and most other observers by surprise. It was not logical that a new bull market would begin 2 months after the 1929 peak.

THE LENGTH OF BEAR MARKETS

History shows that bear markets tend to last a third to half as long as their preceding bull market. Two months would seem to have been an impossibly short period for a full correction of the long bull market, even though the DJIA had suffered a 50% correction at that 1929 low. As was the first drop in 1987. The tip off in 1987 that the market was not readying for a further plunge was the "dullness" which followed, which I discussed in Chapter 6.

But hindsight is easy. When we are living through an event, using tools to predict what will happen next is not so easy. All the market tools in the world will not enable you to precisely call every top and bottom. But they will help you be right far more often than you are wrong.

MORE ON SHORT INTEREST

Another word about short interest during bear markets. As we said earlier, the shorts are not to be looked at as a big support factor in bear times. Let's look at the short interest figures of the 1929–32 crash.

The first short interest figure ever issued by the New York Stock Exchange was on May 25, 1931. It was 5.5 million shares. The Dow Jones stood at 130 then. By December, it fell to 73 (nearly 50%). The shorts had made a killing, and, by the end of the year, the short interest dropped to 2.8 million shares.

A rally then carried through to March 1932. The short interest rose to 3.5 million in January 1932 and to 3.3 at the rally peak in March. Then, the market went into its worst percentage decline in history (March to July 1932). Again, the shorts were correct.

It seems to me that, during a bear market (following a great and active bull market), we can expect to have a continuing large short interest. But this does not mean the shorts must lose money. During a bull market, nobody asks how all those buyers can be right! Yet, during a bear market, one constantly hears that "all those shorts must be wrong."

This strongly suggests the position of the short seller during an extended bear market is a vastly different thing from the position of the short seller during a primary bull market.

10
Cycles Study: A Useful Market Tool?

From time to time, even very respectable analysts project our entire future based on some fairly precise cycle theory.

For example, the theories of the Russian economist Nikolai Kondratieff have been dusted off by several analysts. For those of you not familiar with the *Kondratieff Wave*, it purports to see a regular set of long-term cycles beginning in the late 18th century, and projected forward into the future. Kondratieff's studies were a product of the 1920s and 1930s when many economists, including John Maynard Keynes, were imbued with the idea that objective knowledge about historical change could be projected into the future as an inductive science.

Since Kondratieff formulated his theories, they have been used to predict that the 1930s' Depression would go even lower than it did. To predict that, first, the early 1970s and, then, the early 1980s would dissolve into massive worse-than-1930s-style depressions. Even though these predictions didn't come to pass, Kondratieff was resurrected again in 2001. The desire for life "formulas" is strong.

Faith that the future is mathematically measurable is so seductive that even after a cycles theory has been proven not to work, when things begin to look uncertain and the need for stability is great, the failures of past cycles prognostication are forgotten.

But life is not a mathematically recurring phenomenon. It's a dynamic evolving process. Because of this, it is very difficult to equate any past era with our own with precision.

Most cycles go back at least 100 years. But how can one compare the price of wheat in the days of the horse-driven plow with the price of wheat in the days of computerized farms? What resemblance is there between the price of a TV and a phonograph, or a computer and a quill pen? Exact comparisons are impossible. I am not saying that we should ignore all cycles study, rather that we should be wary of anybody claiming that a particular cycle is the key to the future.

WAVES NOT CYCLES

David Hackett Fisher wrote a fascinating book in 1996 on long-term price revolutions. But he does not call his work "Cycles." Instead the title is: *The Great Wave*. And though he traces waves back to the 12th century, if you are looking for exact cycles you will come away from his book very disappointed.

He agrees that life is a dynamic process and any recurrence in human events that can be detected is more akin to waves hitting a shore than a wheel describing an exact cyclical path over and over. But that does not mean all cycles practitioners are wrong. Indeed, there are some very good market analysts who use Elliott Wave Theory, Fibonacci number series, and even Astrology to predict where markets might go to next.

But if their batting average is good, and if they are honest, they will admit that they also keep technical indicators, use chart patterns and many of the tools described in this book to complete their prognostications. And they use that most important tool of all, which can only be self-taught: they have a "feel" for markets, developed over years of experience.

Cycles study has its place as yet another market tool. But only for use in conjunction with other market tools, certainly not as a magic bullet.

OUR CURRENT AGE IS VERY DIFFERENT

The main factor that has changed the whole equation and concept of economic cycles in our own times began with the desk-top computer. Though the computer was invented in 1946, it was not until the early 1980s that they could be made small enough and inexpensive enough for them to be widely used. Governments can now influence economies more acutely than ever before.

We may never see a German Weimar-style inflation again, nor the deflation of the 1930s. They could more easily occur in the days when it took a long time to gather statistics together in a central location; then armies of accountants and economists had to digest, analyze, and interpret those figures using only manual tools. By the time the economists had compiled the data and had suggestions about what to do, many statistics were already out of date. And the problem, whatever it was, was already out of control.

But the bad side of the ability to influence an economy with the help of computers is that governments really believe they can create prosperity and almost eliminate the natural rise and fall of prices that occurs in any free market society. This lulls the public into a sense that acute risk is *no longer involved* when they invest, and prods governments to tinker ever more fervently with the economy, when their prior efforts didn't work.

Economies can be government influenced in a mild way, without huge damage. But if governments try to control them in a major way, and thus defy the tides of a free, dynamic society, the net result will be more dramatic fluctuation. Instead of a quick sharp bear market to squeeze out excesses, of the sort we saw in 1981 when government for once did the right thing, we will see a steady deterioration, where not only the economy suffers but the dynamism of society is eroded.

THE THEORY OF CHAOS, WHICH ISN'T CHAOTIC AT ALL, JUST DYNAMIC

The more we learn about computers, the more we realize how much we don't know. In the early 1960s, meteorologist Edward Lorenz developed a re- markable set of equations that could only be used on a computer, which in turn led to what is now known as Chaos Theory. Stated simply, it says that the movement of the wings of a butterfly in Beijing can cause a tornado in Kansas.

What that means is that our world is so delicately and intricately structured that any deviation from the norm, however minor, has a ripple effect through the entire system—any system, magnifying it as it goes. It doesn't mean that we live in a chaotic world. Rather, that it is impossible to predict anything exactly, because in order to predict exactly you need an infinite amount of information about the initial conditions. This leads us to two conclusions:

1.   Chaos Theory demonstrates that cycles only work in very general ways.
2.   Governments should stop pretending they have all the facts necessary to create prosperity and get out of the way and allow the economy to go through its natural ups and downs, which will make for a lot less bumpy and corrosive ride.

CYCLES CAN WORK WITHIN LIMITATIONS

But there are parallels one can draw from the past that are valid for the future, though they must be modified to fit the context of the modern world and not be superimposed blindly.

Human *reaction* to events tends to be similar in similar circumstances. Structures and equipment have limits to how far they can be pushed, and beyond that limit spells danger. For example, if you own a horse and buggy and you drive the horse until he drops without food, you have lost your transportation. If you drive your car until it runs out of gas, you are in the same predicament. But, if you then say that past cycles in the price of hay can equate to the price of oil, you are pushing the idea of cycles too far. Life isn't that simplistic.

We do learn from the past. But Cycles Theory suggests that we keep making the same mistakes over and over. If this were true, life expectancy would still be around 40 years, and we would still condone child factory labor and lynch-mob justice.

One reason we have not eliminated bear markets and recessions is not because we keep making the same mistakes over and over, but because, as we advance technologically, the problems we need to solve may be similar in a general sense, but they pop up with a different face and in a different context. If all bear markets *looked* exactly alike, we would cope better and faster. It is because each one, though bearing some resemblance to past bears, is unique, that we miss some of the road signs.

People's reactions to boom and bust are fairly predictable based on precedent. But the *details* of how they will react, and how long it will take them to react depends on communications, whether newscasts are biased, and how informed and aware they are.

Therefore the assumption that human affairs operate in mathematically predictable time patterns is just not true. There are fairly predictable sequences, but time is one aspect impossible to forecast. There is an old Wall Street adage which states that the market always does what it is supposed to do, but never when it is supposed to.

DOORS TO CYCLES STUDY

Do not, however, dismiss the findings of those who study cycles. Their research is useful to market analysis. If you study their statistics, you will often find that they have indeed found certain vague recurring patterns in human behavior. It is just that they push it too far and insist that there is a mathematical 9.3-year cycle in grasshopper plagues or computer sales, instead of looking behind the recurring event to discover what *caused* fluctuations in business or natural cycles at that time, and then try to find a modern equivalent reason.

History does repeat itself up to a point, but, when the rerun occurs, it comes clothed in such different attire we almost never recognize it.

TO SUM UP

If you try to use cycles exactly, you will miss the wood for the trees. But, if you use the fact that human events tend to recur because we *react* to similar situations in similar ways, you have at your disposal a very valuable tool in the bear war.

11
Chart Reading and Interpretation

"Pride of opinion caused the downfall of more men on Wall Street than all the other opinions put together."

Charles H. Dow

DOW THEORY

Is Dow Theory old-fashioned? Sure, just like a communications satellite. It still works, almost as well as ever, in bear market or bull. Those who dismiss Dow Theory expect it to behave like any other technical tool. But that was not what Charles Dow had in mind when he created the Averages. His first experiment to create an average that would offer a broad perspective of American business and the economy was made up of 11 stocks, mainly railroad companies. But, during the next couple of years, it became clear to him that railroads did not present a complete picture of the US economy. The new industrial companies, which in the late 19th century were considered as speculative as the Internet companies were in the late 20th century, were nonetheless, in Dow's estimation, a major contributor to America's growth. And the products made by the new industrial companies were being delivered by the railroads, so in 1896 the Dow Jones Industrial Averages and the Dow Jones Railroad Averages were created. Today, the transportation index acts in the same way that the old railroad index did.

Dow Theory was seen as a bellwether indicator of *economic direction*, rather than a stock market predictor. But, over the 100 plus years it has been in existence, it has forecast most major bull and bear markets. The transportation average still needs to confirm the Industrials. It's the oldest theory on Wall Street and one of the few that have stood the test of time. Dow Theory holds that whenever the DJIA moves to a new rally high (or low), the Dow Jones transportation average must do the same (thus "confirming the move") shortly thereafter, or else the move is false and cannot long be sustained and a reversal will follow. And vice versa, if the transportation average makes the first move.

When the averages hold above the preceding low points, it is construed bullishly; when they fail to climb above preceding highs, it is said to be a bearish signal. Further, the theory holds that the market is forecasting business and that the market surges in three movements. And it has much to say about how volume must act, during the penetrations referred to above. For more details on Dow Theory, I would recommend you read *Technical Analysis of Stock Trends*, by Edwards and Magee (listed in the Resources section of this book). But to become expert on Dow Theory is virtually a lifetime study, and few have done just that. The man, in my view, who is most capable of Dow interpretation today is my friend Richard Russell.

CRITICISMS

Critics of Dow Theory during the 1990s said that the transportation index is no longer relevant or, at best, is so insignificant it is not required to confirm the action of the dynamic average. There were even suggestions that a new Dow Theory should be created, to compare the "old economy" with the so-called "new economy." As a rebuff, I would point out that, although many Nasdaq stocks collapsed in 2000, it was only when the airlines (transportation companies) began to falter in the aftermath of the September 11, 2001 attack that even the talking heads on television began seriously to talk about recession. In spite of the criticism, Dow Theory was alive and well and pointed to a bear market long before September 11, 2001.

A LAGGING SIGNAL

Because Charles Dow designed this theory as a forecaster of business, not a predictor of stock action, confirmation of signals tends to be coincident or trailing, not leading. However, two points should be raised on that score:

1.   Even if late, it is important to have a confirmation that still occurs soon enough, in most cases, to let you capture a gain or avoid the greatest part of a loss.

2.   If you take partial action based on the first part of an unconfirmed Dow

Signal, which is often recommended if the first signal occurs on good volume and other technical indicators are in gear, then you get in on an even larger share of the move.

Dow also was adamant that bull markets are born when bear markets take values (dividends) *up* and price–earnings (P/E) ratios *down*. Up and down are relative words, so it's a general, not a precise tool. But it's *part* of Dow Theory.

The greatest use for Dow Theory is that confirmation of the two averages tells you the new bull or bear market is a real reflection of the health of the economy, not merely an internal market correction. But, like any market tool, it is not infallible. Its signals on occasion have been too early or too late to be an absolute truth. Experience is important in its interpretation. So, it should be used in conjunction with all the other tools and indicators we discuss in this book.

AVERAGES HAVE CHANGED SHAPE BUT NOT SUBSTANCE

The second Dow Jones average has changed shape considerably since it became the transportation index instead of just the rail average. But its *raison d'être* within Dow Theory remains valid, in that the production of goods and services will not make an economy hum, unless there are efficient ways to get those products to market. In Dow's day, the only way to move goods and people was via the railroads. Today, though we use trucking and airplanes, the principle is the same.

STOCK CHARTS

In a world and stock market full of uncertainties, stock charts offer no guarantee. But, given their limitations, they provide the nearest approach to a stock market road map. In the realm of stock geography, they help you know where you are, where you have been, and where you might go. Charts are factual records of what has occurred, but the chart *reader* makes them come alive, and thus the result depends on his ability, judgment, and instincts alone. Each chart is a picture that speaks a thousand words.

"There's nothing wrong with charts. It's the chart readers who can fail." That bromide is nearly true. Charts can give false signals. They are not fail-safe. There are traps and false moves that even the most perceptive of chartists can miss.

But, in dealing with percentages, it's reasonable to say that a really good chartist makes far more correct forecasts of forthcoming stock action than incorrect ones. Then, if the chartist follows a principle of cutting losses quickly on the bad guesses, overall he will make a good profit.

Before becoming a chart follower, I was happy in my ignorance. But, after my conversion to charting, I could never feel safe in the market again without charts. It would be like starting off on a long trip and finding your map stolen. Charts tell you where to place your orders to buy or sell, based on points where a lot of support or resistance is present owing to past activity at certain levels, or where a stock has formed a pattern from which it has broken up or down.

It is perhaps hard for a generation whose only experience of the stock market was that "buy and hold" was the ultimate in market know-how. But, in today's markets, you need charting methods that have stood the test of decades, and helped chart pioneers navigate through all bear markets of the 20th century.

KEEP YOUR OWN CHARTS

I believe that every investor should keep a chart on each stock he owns or watches. If you devote 1 or 2 hours a day to your indicators and charts, that is enough. If you own more stocks than you have time to either manually chart, or personally analyze from a computer stock chart service, you are too diversified. As stated earlier, if you have never kept charts, at least for the first few months, I suggest you manually keep your own charts, in order to gain a feel for the patterns as they form. When that sense becomes second nature, it's safe to switch to a ready-made chart service. For the average investor (maybe we should say "above average" because hardly anybody in the stock market will ever admit to being only average), we say a dozen or so stock charts will do nicely, plus a dozen market indicators, on a daily and weekly basis. Add monthly if possible.

The rules on how to read a chart properly can be learned only one way. You must read Edwards' and Magee's book, *Technical Analysis of Stock Trends*. It is not an easy read, but the knowledge you gain is worth the effort. You will be encouraged to find that stocks are forming the same patterns today that they did 30 years ago and 60 years ago, and even 90 years ago. In bear markets, there are more of certain patterns, than in bull markets, and vice versa. This has always been so. The rationale is that chart patterns are formed by people's emotional buying and selling patterns. *People patterns* are what you really see on a chart, not stock patterns.

THE BEAUTY OF CHARTS

The trick in the stock market has never been what stock to buy or sell or sell short, but *when*. That's where charts come to the rescue. Charts will guide you in both what to buy and when. Once you have used a chart to buy a stock, it usually gives you a sell target. Then, you watch for possible negative chart patterns to appear that may alter your targeted sell price. During the 1990s, bull market investing was so easy that some, who felt they had made a decent profit and sold, spent the late 1990s complaining that they had missed extra profits they might have made if they had not sold so soon. But, they were grateful in 2000 when the Nasdaq crashed. The investment climate for the next few years is going to be totally different. Taking small profits will probably be the name of the game. In any case, whatever the climate, charts both *protect* you and paint the path to profits.

The beauty of charts is their capability (based on your interpretative ability) to tell both when to buy and when to sell precisely(!), with logical rationale. *Listen* to your charts. If they say buy or sell, don't argue. Charts follow the money. So, follow the charts.

POINT-AND-FIGURE CHARTS

What I have said thus far has been primarily about line-and-bar charts, the type that run a vertical line between the high and low price of a stock, with a short crossbar where the stock closed, and show the volume below the price. But most of my commentary applies equally to point-and-figure charting, which is a different method for achieving similar ends.

Point and figure differs from line and bar in concept in that it plots movement of points only—*without regard to time*. The line-and-bar method takes time as well as volume fully into account.

Point and figure is done on equal-size squared paper (arithmetical graph paper) rather than the semi-logarithmical chart paper that about half the line-and-bar chartists use. And, instead of a line and bar, it records an X or an O in a connected sequence, following price only, not volume. Entries are made vertically and only when the stock moves a full point (or more, depending on the scale). Reversal of price action starts a new column.

Point and figure is less work and takes much less time. But it's harder to get the hang of, and much more difficult to get a mental picture from—for beginners at least—and is not so good for short-term trades. Some say you need to subscribe to a service to get proper figures to post.

LINE-AND-BAR CHARTS

Some who make line-and-bar charts use semi-logarithmical chart paper. It has been highly touted as necessary to "see a move in proper percentage perspective." This is true. But the average investor tends to think in terms of points rather than percentages. If the Dow falls 200 points in a single day, people tend to focus more on the number of points, than on the percentage fall they represent.

Semi-logarithmical charts have their uses, and their distortions. If you have time keep both kinds of chart, particularly for the DJIA or S&P.

CANDLESTICK CHARTS

The third choice—candlestick charts—have become very popular in the West in the last 10 years. They were developed by the Japanese over a century ago to trade rice futures. The name "candlestick" is derived from their appearance on a chart, which resembles a candlestick with a wick (shadow) sticking out of one, or both ends. The basis for candlestick charting is the relationship between the open, high, low, and closing prices for each trading day.

A candlestick supplies two important pieces of information. The thick part of the candlestick, called the body or real body, represents the range between the day's opening and closing price. And the color of the real body indicates direction in relation to the day's opening price. If the body is filled black, it means the close was lower than the open (bearish). If the body is empty (i.e., white), it means the close was higher than the open (bullish). The longer or shorter the real body, the more bearish or bullish the signal given. As bearish bars are filled in black and bullish bars are left empty as white, it is easy to determine the dominating forces in candlestick charts. The thin lines, called shadows, protruding above and below the real body indicate the extreme high and low for the day.

Candlestick chart patterns can be interpreted in the same way as normal bar charts. However, many candlestick formations involving groups of candlesticks are unique to their discipline and must be interpreted via the rules associated with this oriental art.

BENEFITS DEPEND ON YOU

The benefits of *looking* at a charted index or charts of stocks and market averages are different for each person for the reason cited by Georg Christoph Lichenberg long ago when he said, "A book [or chart] is a mirror; if a donkey peers into you, you can't expect an apostle to look out."

Part V
MONEY-MAKING TACTICS

"Money is like a sixth sense—and you can't make use of the other five without it."

Somerset Maugham

12
Preservation of Capital during a Bear Market

"Solvency is entirely a matter of temperament and not of income."

Logan Pearsall Smith, 1931

During the 1990s, increasing one's capital was "the thing," and the simple preservation of capital was considered old-fashioned. But, as I have already discussed in prior chapters, no matter whether the future brings bull or bear markets, the kind of euphoric and wild bull market we witnessed during the 1980s and 1990s is unlikely to happen again—for at least the next decade or so. Though this book is concerned mainly with bear market tactics, what I will discuss in this chapter applies to future bull markets as well.

Preservation of capital is primary. Profits are acutely important but secondary, and, before you make any investment decision, you should first ascertain the risk inherent in that investment vehicle and decide in your own mind what the worst possible outcome could be. Only when you have gone through this type of "risk reflection," can you make an informed decision of whether the particular investment is right for you. The human condition is to look at "best case" not worst case.

ACTING ACCORDING TO THE STAGE OF THE MARKET

The strategy key is to be found in determining what "stage" of the market you are in. Thus, if you are well along in the last stage of a bull market, you sell out your common stock holdings across the board, even though you are "rather sure" the market averages still have some upside distance ahead though with fewer stocks on board, as is typical for bull market endings. If you get greedy and reach for the precise top, you'll more often regret it.

SQUEEZING OUT PROFITS

The manner of selling out should be normally via stop-loss orders, set in accordance with the stock's short-term uptrend line. Often, this will be from 5 to 15% below the current price. It's necessary to look at a daily chart to do this properly, and the extra profits are worth the extra trouble.

If you find that your indicators suddenly point to the "*early* stage" of the bear market, you may just sell out, without stop-loss orders. By the time you have recognized "*all*" the signs, it may be rather late and you will wish you had sold sooner. Emotionally, you'll wonder if it isn't "too late to sell now."

But, if you believe you are in the "*middle* stage" of a bear market (which comprises the major portion of all bear markets), then you lean heavily on your technical tools or indicators to determine if, at that moment, they point to a secondary reaction (up). My chapters on market tools and secondary reactions will aid in making this determination.

ACTION IN THE ADVANCED OR MIDDLE STAGE OF A BEAR MARKET

If such a secondary reaction is *already under way*, you have several choices:

1.   Sell in stages what you hold long, using your technical tools to gauge the top of the up-move. This you must do if you rate capital preservation high. The top of a secondary reaction (up) in most bear markets offers the highest prices that will be seen for probably 1 to 5 years. This is because the bear market "assumedly" has time left to run, after which it will normally remain dormant awhile, then slowly build up to a new bull market, all of which takes time. The prices on this reaction will be the best you can hope for, even though they may look pitifully low to you, since they had been so much higher 6–12 months before.

Even the long-term investor must get out here. We are not dealing with certainties in the stock market (or in any other phase of life) but with probabilities, and you can't afford the risk of going against the probabilities here. The odds favor lower prices are long. And for a long time.

This "choice" sounds easy on paper, but in practice it's agonizingly difficult. Why? Because, as the rally mounts, the talk will be that the bear market is over, or that we are starting a new bull market, or that maybe it wasn't really a bear market anyway. Some will say the DJIA is going 500 points higher in the next

30 days. Volume will probably mount. Some good business news will be available. Most brokers will be bullish and urge customers to buy. You will be torn between the stage scenery (those 500 points especially) and what you are pretty sure is backstage.

But experience teaches that those extra 500 points are a mirage most of the time. If you like only short odds in your favor, then stick around. Maybe you'll be lucky.

"Each man must kill his own snakes," as Robert Rhea once said of stock market decisions. This book can tell you where the snakes are, but you have to take the action yourself, and it's never, never easy. Only on paper is it easy. Partly, that's because we live only 1 day at a time, whereas on paper we can span 6 months in a paragraph.

In this situation, we again face what we discussed in the chapter on human psychology in the stock market. Winning in the market is largely a matter of fighting a battle within yourself. Intellectual domination of your emotions will win the day, if it is indeed won. The majority will fail to win the day, for the majority cannot, or will not, try to control their emotions. So, this simple choice of "selling on the rally" will prove a massive barrier to you unless you develop nerves of steel and act against what some of your emotions are coaxing you to do.

You must ignore both profits and losses, and forsake what appear to be probable profits ahead, and sell when the signs say so.

The most difficult part of all is not to let your bullish emotions, in a rally, cause you to make rose-colored *interpretations* of an indicator. For example, if the number of daily "new highs" fails to exceed the "new lows" (or does so only moderately) during a rally, you will be tempted to discount it (because subconsciously you want to hide such evidence under the rug). You may say, "Well, you've got to expect the highs to be fewer because the market is well down from its peak." So much for this "simple" choice number one.

2.   Buy a few stocks that look bullish on their charts (see Chapter 11 on charts), as perhaps 10 to 25% of total stocks may, if it is not too far along in the intermediate term, up-move (i.e., the secondary reaction in a bear market). Thus, you'll get a nice play for several points profit, assuming you have done your chart reading properly. You should pick stocks that have little apparent downside risk and good support levels: stocks that are in a new uptrend and enjoy increased volume, and perhaps have something fundamentally bright.

Sometimes, the blue chips are best on secondary rallies; sometimes, the low-price stocks; sometimes, the cyclicals or the utilities. No two situations can be the same, and that's why I advocate making your selection on the basis of *chart* action. The charts tell you which group is strongest and/or which are making reversal patterns. It will usually be a "logical" group to advance, based on conditions at that stage of the economy or market. Watch the volume leaders for candidates.

That may not seem appropriate for preservation of capital, but in truth it is, provided you do not invest too heavily in this stage. It's like Napoleon's advice that to attack is the best defense. One must go with the trend, even the short or medium-term trend at times. Probably 25 to 30% should be your maximum commitment in this period. There is always the risk that you have not made correct interpretations of the signs of the times and the technical tools, and what you calculate to be an intermediate-term rally may in fact be a primary reversal; thus, some investment in it will be welcome.

If, for the "buy and hold" crowd, this sounds like peculiar advice, let me quote part of friend John Templeton's strategy that created his huge fortune. Even at the height of the 1990s' bull market, he never mentally, or emotionally, put all his money in stocks. His "buy and hold" portion of his portfolio was only ever 50%. The other 50% was sometimes in bonds or defensive issues, if he felt doubtful about the trend. That's a good strategy to adopt.

But, because Templeton is a multi-millionaire, he could afford to risk a higher percentage of his assets than most people.

However, in good conscience, the best advice for *ultra-conservative* preservation of capital is to participate in these contra-trend moves in *closed-end* mutual funds.

Holding this type of share lets you sleep better, doesn't make you quite such a devotee to your charts, and doesn't subject you to the whims of news and the hype that most TV newscasters use to keep you watching and their sponsors happy. You don't make nearly as much profit this way, but, on a normal intermediate secondary reaction (up), you should make enough points to make it worthwhile. If you are also short, this hedges your position nicely.

Even this method, however, is not perfect. At times, some closed-end mutual funds tend to specialize in specific industries and would be the equivalent of buying into just one industry group. So, if you like this fund idea, make sure you know exactly what they are invested in and how diversified they are.

To hold something both long and short is a common practice with many sophisticated investors. If you feel you know charts well enough to pick the strong stocks to hold long and the weak ones to hold short, this is a reasonable approach as you are balanced and invested with *individual* stock trends. Whether you buy a mutual fund or a stock is obviously an individual choice, based on how much risk you want to absorb and how far you have progressed in your study of market trends and chart analysis. You pay your money and you take your chance.

3.   Sell short at the top (you hope) of the rally (secondary reaction). Although this possibility is the most profitable of the lot, it's against your nature and the one you're least likely to want to do (see Chapter 13

on short-selling techniques). Not only is it difficult psychologically for most people to sell short, but it's made doubly difficult by the fact that it should be done when prices are still inching up—or just beginning to slip a bit; whereas the odd lotter/amateur will only have the courage to sell short when the specter of a crash triggers his mental "fear" screen, which is usually when the down leg is almost over.

Selling short as soon as prices start to dip is much safer, for you can rest assured by all stock market history that even bull market up phases have reactions. The big bonus is that shorting near what appears a rally top enables you to place a logical stop-loss order very *near* your short-sell price at above the rally peak. The longer you wait, the bigger that gap. So, a short in a bear market is more likely to make a profit and with less risk placed at this immediate post-rally stage, than after prices have been falling for some days.

But even shorting late in the game is not fatal because, if you are in a bear market, prices must eventually go lower, even if there is another rally soon after you sell short. You can in theory wait it out, just as you do in bull markets when you buy a stock, and then the stock turns down. You then wait for the market to come back and make you well. But, success in this case depends on how much heat you can stand. A stop is necessary in either case.

I'll discuss stop-loss orders again in the short-selling chapter (Chapter 13), but let me say that stops give you peace of mind, especially when you are new at shorting. Later on, you may use them or not as you prefer, depending on how close you are to the market.

4.   Selling out and *staying out* is the fourth course of action. This choice is one rarely practiced; yet, it contains wisdom for *some* people. But, then, that's the hallmark of wisdom, something not widely known or, if known, not widely practiced. When you find a rally (secondary reaction type) about to start or already under way in a bear market and you have sold out (as per choice 1 above), then you need not follow choices 2 or 3, but take this opt-out choice instead. You need not either go long to make a few points or short on the rally high, since both involve some risk and both require much attention to indicators. You can simply play it safe by selling out and then staying out, putting your money in Treasury bonds or other defensive fixed-interest paper. Or, in the case of an inflationary bear market, in "tangible investments"— gold, real estate, art, etc.

The act of staying out is just as much a positive action as buying or selling, and, in fact, requires more courage at times. Robert Rhea, in 1937's bear market, wrote: "A bear market is a good time for a vacation, and I am taking one."

Or, another way to put it: "Often, riding at anchor is the best course." This choice depends on your self-analysis. Are you temperamentally suited to shorting? Can you apply yourself to indicators, tools, charts? Will you be unhappy out of the market—doing nothing as you watch the action? You alone can answer these questions. You may not know the answer till you study more, or paper trade, or try your hand with bear market strategies.

5.   Never go against the trend. We can call this choice 5 or give it a subheading under choice 3. (It's not important how you categorize them, just so you incorporate them into your thinking.) This calls for never going against the trend. It means that you go short only until you see a secondary (up) reaction at hand. Then, you cover your shorts and stay out until the turndown starts again. Then, you short again. You keep shorting and covering, shorting and covering. Never going long, only short. Thus, you never buck the "major" trend. And you are never in the market during major rallies, which, it must be admitted, are tricky affairs in bear markets, and thus you avoid the risk of being "whipsawed."

SUMMARY

So much for the choices in a middle area of the bear market. I summarize them by saying you should sell out (on a secondary rally); you should buy a few stocks long (for a secondary rally); you ought to go short if you want to cash in on the bear; and/or, if you want to be very safe, you will sell out and stay out.

ACTION IN THE LATE STAGE OF A BEAR MARKET

If you find yourself in the *late* stage of a bear market, and have confirmed it thoroughly with both signs of the times and the technical tools, your choices are simplified. You know that you are going to be buying soon. You have only to decide when and what you should buy.

The *when* means: "Shall I buy now and collect dividends while I wait for the usually lengthy simmering period before a new bull market begins, or do I wait until it has actually begun rising?" This decision is facilitated by asking yourself what you will do with your money if you wait. If you have no better place for it, it may as well be collecting dividends (while you keep checking your market indicators).

The *what* means you don't just buy any stock that looks healthy; you pick those that traditionally (not certainly, mind you) rise *fastest* in the first phase of a bull market. This usually means low-priced stocks or, if you want to be more conservative, the low-priced medium-quality stocks. Blue chips normally come later. Watch for "relative strength" of individual stocks and groups.

PEACE OF MIND

And, for all stages of both bull and bear markets, you should "Take a View" (which we discussed in Chapter 3). It helps to know the overall context in which your technical tools give you their signals. Taking a View requires, however, that you pay more than a little attention to non-technical indicators, to make it possible to take a long enough look ahead to make your view a sound one. Then, check your view each week to see that nothing has changed in the superstructure of the world economy.

This sounds simple, but it takes practice and discipline. The greatest rules and truths are always simple things. But they are rarely appreciated and even less often followed. Charles Poore put it well when he wrote, "There is nothing quite so complicated as simplicity. Infinitudes of distractions and irrelevancies must be forced into perspective to achieve it." Golden words!

CONCLUSIONS

Whatever stock market you invest in, the tactics remain the same. As communications get ever better, so all world markets tend to rise or fall together, though the degree of difference is critical. And it is now possible to trade your account, from anywhere to anywhere.

Perhaps the most important tactic in any kind of market anywhere is to get rid of your weakest investments, hold your strongest, cut your losses quickly, use stops, and leave your better-acting securities alone until they bring comfortable profits. This sounds like just plain common sense, but, because of our emotions, we quite often do the opposite.

A CAUTION

The long and medium-term investor should use almost identical techniques in bear markets. I have never been convinced that the long-term investor is fully justified in "riding out" reactions. Yes, sometimes, the investor is saved from the 100-point fall by an eventual equal rise, but one can never be sure how long the market will take to come back or indeed how low it will go before it does come back. Thus, it is my personal view that, during a bear market, the interests and tactics of the long, medium, and short-term investor should be virtually the same.

13
Short Selling 101

When I discuss "the business" with other advisory service owners, they tell me that it is difficult to sell their publications unless they advise buys, or to a *much* lesser degree a few sells, but in almost no case, sell shorts! (There are a few services who suggest shorts, usually balanced by longs, but they are a mere handful, and even they would experience tough going if they were to advise only shorting for prolonged periods.)

Bear markets are bad times for investment advisory services, owing to public psychology. This is sad because there is big money to be made on the short side. But the public is not short-sell minded. We advise a toe-to-the-water approach. Try it slowly and see. It's not so cold. In fact, it's fine once you get in. You gain confidence that you can handle *any* market direction!

But know the ropes first. In theory, short selling can cost you more (because a stock you buy at $20 can only go to zero, but a stock you sell short at 20 can go to 60 or 400). But, if you follow the strategies outlined in this chapter, this would never happen to you. A simple stop-loss order gives total protection. Short selling in a bear market is "investing with the trend," so no one should be afraid of it.

SHORT SELLING DEFINED

I will keep definitions and descriptions of shorting to a minimum because the intricacies of shorting tend to confuse people and add nothing of value to their knowledge, for it doesn't matter how the mechanics are done. If you just accept the fact that they are done automatically by your broker, it will be easier for you.

However, for those who must have it spelled out and who expect it in a book on bear markets, I include the following minimum procedural explanation. A short sale is one in which borrowed securities are used for delivery to the buyer (in the transaction in which you sell short). The process is not complete until the seller discharges his obligation to the lender by delivering to him the securities to cover the short sale.

Many will not grasp how they can sell what they do not own. It is possible because of your broker's facilities for borrowing stocks with which he is able to make delivery for you. When you sell short and your broker has borrowed a portion of stock and delivered it to the purchaser, the first part of the transaction is complete.

COVERING THE SHORT

As with all trades, there remains the second half, that of covering your short. That is, providing your broker with an equivalent amount of stock at a later date so he can return it to the person or broker from whom he borrowed it (which you do by telling him to "buy to cover" the short).

But you can take your sweet time about this second half of the deal. Unlike if you buy a put option (which in simplified terms is a highly leveraged short sale), when you have a specific date by which you must exercise your option, you don't have to cover your short sale in *any* specified time period. In theory, this can be many years. There is no time limit, provided your account is in good order.

Under US laws, short sales are only possible on upticks, which means the stock must move up $\frac{1}{8}$ of a point, after reaching your short-sell price, to be executed. If a stock *only* moves down, you'll never get short in it. (Laws vary from country to country.)

So, you get an execution. They credit your account with the proceeds of the amount of shares you have sold short at the price at which you shorted it, just as in any other sale of stock. Now, let's say that stock dropped 10 points. You decided that was low enough and you wanted to take a profit. You called your broker and said, "Buy 100 *XYZ* to cover my short at 45 or better." In this case, "or better" means or less.

Let's say an execution is made at 44. Now, ignoring the commissions, you made 11 points. You sold at 55 and later bought at 44. It's just the opposite of buying at 44 and selling at 55.

SHORT-SELLING TACTICS

But I believe short sales should always be protected with a stop-loss order so that if it does not immediately go as you planned, you are out with, say, a 10–15% loss (based on the chart) and that's the end of it. No nightmares, no big risks. From bitter experience, I've learned that the time to place a stop-loss order is the day you *take* a new position in a stock. At that point, you can do it objectively. Later, you start rationalizing. And, often, "later" never comes. So, put in the stop-loss order the same day you short. However, the chart pattern may change and alter the best place for a stop, so never just place a stop and forget about it.

The stop-loss order on a short sale is just the same as on a long position, only in reverse. You order the stock bought if it goes up to a certain price. As a matter of tactics, I would warn against shorting after a stock has fallen sharply. Chances are always good that the stock will rally after a sharp fall, whether or not it later falls again. And that rally would either scare you out or hit your stop-loss order; either one causes you an unnecessary loss.

The time to short is at the start of the fall, based usually on its chart pattern and/or perhaps on your analysis that the market as a whole is due for a fall.

SELECTING STOCKS TO SHORT

Great care should be exercised in picking stocks to short to get the "most mileage" for your position. Stay away from stocks with a small number of shares outstanding. Avoid stocks that already have so many people short in them that the situation can boomerang. (See financial pages for a list of short sales, on approximately each 20th of the month.)

I generally stick to shorting blue chips. That may sound dangerous, but in reality they are the safest, for they are heavily traded. The Nasdaq offers more tempting and profitable shorts, but only the nimblest of traders (and chartists) are at home there.

Short selling is a tricky business, but those in a position to do a little homework can weed out the most logical candidates for profitable shorting especially during bear markets. Our number-one rule for short sellers is: Short positions should be protected against more than a 10–15% loss with a "stop-buy" order placed with your broker at the time you make the short sale.

To select the best shorts—charts are a "must"—make use of one of the bar chart services (see Resources chapter for names). Go through their charts and make a list of the stocks that meet some of the requirements listed below.

Don't just do it on screen, online. Print out charts from a chart service. You need paper charts in hand to enable you to properly compare stocks with one another, and draw in lines and curves:

1.   The stock had a large rise in recent weeks or months—preferably, an emotional rise not founded on reality.
2.   The rise was on increased volume, implying that many people will rush to sell to protect their paper profits when the stock starts breaking down.
3.   It seems to have stopped rising.
4.   It shows a top area of distribution (large volume at the top, but unable to rise any higher) and recently has started "breaking down" (falling below the top area).
5.   It has not declined more than 10–15% from its secondary peak as yet.
6.   The stock now has an abnormally high P/E ratio.
7.   The stock should have a relatively low short interest.
8.   Avoid stocks too thinly capitalized, as the small supply can make them run up too fast during a rally. It also means illiquidity when you want to cover.
9.   It's desirable if a stock has risen to heavy overhead supply, and ideally to a point where it broke support earlier.

Once you have made up a list of stocks containing some of the above characteristics, give preference to the ones that:

- show greatest downside volatility in past chart action;
- are in industries on the downgrade;
- have just completed a very bearish chart pattern such as a "double top" or "head-and-shoulders";
- are very popular, widely traded.

To traders, there is nothing more satisfying than having a good short position in a bear market, because stocks fall *much faster* than they rise, and in many cases a good short may be held for the long pull if it is in a long major down-trending chart pattern. Novices are advised to delay shorting till they experiment on paper first, to get completely oriented to the technique.

One final rule: Once you have a profit, move your stop down and keep it moving as the price falls (a trailing "stop-buy" order).

RELATIVE STRENGTH

In a bear market or downtrend that you assume may be a bear market, it is vital to study the (up) reactions. Stocks that rally *least* on such upswings are probably the best candidates for shorting. They are low in relative strength to the market as a whole or to their industry group.

The same thing is true when you buy stocks long. Relative strength should also be watched to help determine when to cover a short. Relative strength can be calculated easily. If a stock falls from 30 to 27, it has fallen 3 points, which is 10% (of 30). If at the same time the market average falls from 10,000 to 8,500, it has fallen 15%. So, in this example, the stock was stronger than the market, because it fell less.

You should favor holding or buying stocks that are stronger than the market. You should consider selling or shorting stocks that are weaker than the market. Gauge both by this relative strength concept.

THE MATH OF SHORTING

It is true that the mathematics of shorting is unfavorable regarding the percentage of profit made on capital required, comparing, for example, a stock rising from 100 to 150 with a stock falling from 150 to 100.

But, the fact remains that shorting can be infinitely more profitable if measured in time. The crash phases of bear markets are swift, and shorts make a faster killing. Fortunes can be amassed in days or even hours in a disintegrating market.

WATCH VOLUME

The Wall Street axiom, "Never sell a dull market short during a bull market," can be used in reverse in bear markets, as, "Always sell a dull market short during a bear market." Dull, here, means low volume.

WHY BEARS PROFIT

As said above, the reason bigger profits are possible in bear markets than in bull is that, on average, prices move faster (i.e., in a shorter time). Loosely speaking, over the last 22 bear markets, prices have fallen fast and sharp, while most bull markets see prices move up more slowly over a longer time. Of course, there are exceptions, but they are few.

And the panic phases or crash phases of bear markets are the most profitable of all. There, you can often see the market drop 15 to 25% in a few days. This almost never happens on the upside. Obviously, this offers the biggest potential gain possible in any kind of market. When the *averages* drop 20%, it means the *majority* of stocks are dropping 40% and the more speculative stocks 60%.

Thus, you can make a fortune in just one bear market, in fact in just one crash phase of just one bear market.

Bull markets normally require years of patient trading to build a fortune. But a bear market crash can gain you big profits in a matter of days or weeks.

BEAR RALLIES ARE SHARP

One note of caution, which I deal with further in the next chapter. When you are short, remember that rallies in bear markets are traditionally sharp, which means they can be frightening to bear positions. Be prepared, psychologically, for this, *and use stop-buy orders*.

LEARN BY DOING

After you try paper trading, the real test to learn short selling in the stock market is by doing. Just as you didn't get the feel of the market until you bought your first stock, so too you will not get a feel for shorting (and overcome your fears of it) until you take your first short position. Once in, you'll find (we hope) "the water's fine" (provided you don't forget the stop loss).

I do not wish to minimize the risk of losses that might occur from short sales that are *not* protected by stop-loss orders (which are really "buy-stop" orders) placed above the market.

To repeat, these orders are so placed that the short seller can calculate the possible loss before placing a short sale in motion. But this gives peace of mind, for you know that if the action does not go as expected, the loss is going to be minimal and predetermined.

No one can deny that more money has been lost on Wall Street via long purchases than via shorting.

THE 1990s WERE UNIQUE

The latter part of the 1990s was a time when almost every investor made money in that trending market. But, as times get ever more turbulent, only those who can cross the crowd and be flexible will make money. Since the crowd (or public) is predominantly and almost perpetually invested on the bull side, it will benefit the trader to know when to act with the successful minority. The minority includes, in bear markets, a sizable portion of short sellers.

ILLOGICAL TO STAY LONG

To stay long of stocks during a bear market for "income purposes" is illogical, not to mention costly. The purpose of investment is, first, to protect your capital from loss in either amount or value, and, second, to secure an adequate return in line with the risk involved. To protect capital from depreciation, one must be alert to spot trend changes and quickly exit the long side, regardless of the current dividends being paid on stock, your need for income, or vague hopes that this downturn will be short lived.

You must be willing to sell stocks that show substantial profits, regardless of the need for income from them, if you determine the bull market is exhausted and a change of trend seems at hand.

It is logical for the investor to sell early in a bear trend, and allot a small portion of the proceeds for selling short, and into hedge funds, while putting money you can't afford to risk into defensive issues such as bonds, preferreds, utilities, Muni's, or, in the case of an inflationary bear market, bonds and tangible assets. Even living off capital at such times is cheaper in the long run than holding stocks that decline.

This investor may not be able to bring himself to sell stocks short. But one who sells out during bear markets "sells the situation short" anyhow by accepting cash in advance of an era when *cash is king* and stocks erode in value.

LIMIT YOUR SHORT ORDERS

When you place an order to sell short, it is usually best to place it with a specific *price limit*. Otherwise, if you guess right that the stock is about to fall, it may fall quite a distance before a market order can be executed, in accordance with the uptick rule. Usually, the market and individual stocks show some minor weakness before they enter a crash or violent fall phase, so it is during this modest weakness period that a short order can best be placed.

An "at the market" order should be used mainly when it's time to cover your short, and not an occasion for shaving an extra half-point.

PLAN AHEAD

It is wise to plan ahead in the matter of selection of stocks to be shorted when the time is right. A campaign should be formulated. Watch stocks that fail to hit highs when others in their industry group do, or fail to rally as much and fall more (relative weakness). Use Stochastics to help your timing—it measures overbought and oversold conditions.

THE MORALITY OF SHORTING

A chapter on short selling is not complete without a bit on the matter of the "morality" of shorting. Many people instinctively feel there is something indecent about it. But, when the facts are clearly brought to light, opposition to it disappears. Napoleon, for example, thought short selling in the French Bourse was unpatriotic. But Gaudin explained to Napoleon that those who did so were "expressing their *judgment* of future events," and "not their wish" for the country.

After the September 11, 2001 attack, John LaFalce of the House Financial Services Committee wrote to the Securities and Exchange Commission (SEC) demanding that it consider inhibiting short selling. The sentiment is understandable, in that certain members of terrorist organizations apparently made money for their networks, in advance of September 11, anticipating the panic their attack would cause. These people are criminals, and should be punished to the full extent of the law. But their crime, evil though it was, was insider trading, not short selling. And inhibiting the ability to short by legitimate investors would destabilize markets much more than allowing free markets to operate. Short sellers provide much needed liquidity to markets by creating a cushion of potential buyers during a period when the last thing on the average investor's mind is buying shares.

Making short selling illegal was in fact tried for short periods in Germany during their monetary chaos of the 1920s and 1930s. But, each time it was tried, it was rapidly seen that the absence of short selling made for more turbulent markets, so the prohibition against shorting was repealed. It is because shorts *have* to cover sooner or later, that they help a falling market.

As the market falls, shorts buy to nail down their profits when almost no one else cares to buy. Shorts also buy when rallies scare them. This arrests or lessens the decline. Whenever shorting was ruled illegal, markets were seen to drop as into a bottomless pit.

BEARS UNLOVED

When W.O. Scroggs wrote, "Nobody loves a bear," in 1930, he coined a phrase that has often been used since and has much truth. But it's because of lack of understanding about the good a bear does in maintaining orderly markets that causes that feeling.

In 1932, *The Nation* magazine ran an article called: "Sacred Bulls and Sinister Bears." That typifies the attitude of many, even today, though it is not nearly as bad as it once was. In 1932, W.T. Foster wrote in *The Atlantic Monthly* of "Selling the United States short" in short selling. Often, it seems a bear is unpopular because his success reminds those who have stocks with huge losses from the last bull market how wrong they were.

People never dislike bears in bull markets or when they lose. It is the successful bear that arouses ire. Thus, it is probably little more than natural envy with some very misguided ideas that it is unpatriotic to make money when most of your fellow citizens are losing.

To which I reply, "Free markets and freedom are only possible when citizens are self-reliant, willing to take risks and are solvent." For an investor to willingly lose money, when there are ways for him to make a profit, is silly, unpatriotic, and clueless.

Object to short selling, if you must, on the ground that it is contrary to our natural optimistic spirit, but not on the grounds that it is unethical. And remember, solvent citizens are of more use to society than insolvent ones who then become a burden on others.

ANOTHER DEFENDER OF SHORTING

Edward Meeker also comes to the defense of the short seller in his 1930 book: *The Work of the Stock Exchange*. He points out that when a man buys a stock on margin he is "causing a short sale of money and conversely that every short sale of stock inevitably causes a margin purchase of money."

Then, as now, bears were criticized and depicted as villains, and Meeker defended them as I do today. Meeker said, "The sheer *nonsense* of such statements is apparent to anyone who knows *anything* at all about the stock market, a knowledge which these critics of stock market speculation often hasten to disclaim at the outset."

He also points out that a big bear operator may be able to depress a share price for a time through short selling, but "he can no more destroy intrinsic values than he can lower the temperature by putting ice on the thermometer bulb."

SHORTS SAVE MARKETS

The most impressive testimony ever offered in defense of short sellers was spoken by the president of the New York Stock Exchange in 1914, just before it closed, as World War I had been declared.

Mr Noble said, "A heavy short interest furnished the best safeguard against a sudden and disastrous drop. This short interest was a leading factor in producing the extraordinary resistance in New York which caused so much favorable comment during the few days before the stock exchange closing. It were well if ill-informed people who deprecate short selling would note this fact!"

Further evidence is the dramatic fact that the violence of the 1929 panic can be largely attributed to the remarkably *small* short interest in the market. Even after the first-phase crash, the short interest was found to have been small.

Another NYSE president (Whitney) investigated rumors of tremendous bear raids and reported that short selling "was so small as to be almost inconsequential, being only about one-eighth of 1% of the value of all stocks listed."

HISTORIC OPPOSITION

The question of the legitimacy of short selling is almost as old as the question of speculation itself. A hostile legislative committee investigated short selling in 1913, and the Pujo Committee reported finally that, "there seems no greater reason for prohibiting speculation by way of selling stock in the expectation of buying it back later at lower prices, than by way of purchasing it in anticipation of at once reselling it at higher prices."

Short selling has been misunderstood for decades. It still is. It was forbidden in England in 1733, but the law failed to halt the practice (as most unjust laws do) and it was repealed in 1860. Napoleon I was dissuaded from forbidding it by his finance minister. Later, the French did legislate against it, only to repeal the law after its harmfulness was clearly shown.

New York tried the same experiment and with the same result: banned in 1812, repealed in 1858. These experiments were costly.

It seems to be human nature to condemn short selling, but global history proves that genuine economic benefits result from its use.

14
Strategies for Making Money Even If You Guess Wrong

"A nimble sixpence is better than a slow shilling."

Old English Proverb

Tools, knowledge of market procedure, and economics will help you increase your percentage of right guesses. But, whether you make money at all, or, more importantly, don't lose much when you guess wrong, depends purely on the *tactics* you use.

Practically every tool and piece of knowledge you acquire about the market will give cues of when to buy or sell, or short (i.e., take a position), but only a few give you cues of when to sell or cover your short (i.e., get out of your position). That depends entirely on the tactics you use; and profits are only "paper profits" until you close the transaction.

This method (which works in both bear and bull swings) is notoriously simple, as most great truths are. Even if technical tools or fundamentals fail you, your tactics can save you. And, in conjunction with other things, your tactics can make you tremendous profits. At worst, proper tactics can preserve your capital.

PROFIT FORMULA GIVEN

To illustrate, assume we're in a bear market. You decide it's time to sell short. You need a stock that is moving with the trend (in this case a downtrend). You study the volume leader list published daily. You select a stock that is moving down on heavy volume. You look at its chart. If it's in a suitable downtrend and has some weak fundamentals (lower earnings), and its short interest is not extra large (versus its usual short interest and versus its floating supply of stock), then you place an order to short sell it at a price where it would be rising slightly to touch its downtrend line (unless it happens to be touching it on the day you look at its chart, in which case a market order to sell short would be appropriate).

WATCH THE CHART

If you are not a chart reader and do not have the time or desire to become one, you can probably use this method with the help of a friend or broker who has a knowledge of charts. But, for the purpose of this approach, only the simplest of chart techniques is necessary. I suggest you make your own chart on the stock in which you take a position. A single chart will take only 60 seconds a day to keep up.

One caution. Before you sell it short, be sure the stock chart does not show a "reversal pattern," such as an inverse head and shoulders, or a falling wedge, or a double bottom. Ideally, one tries and hopes to find a chart pattern showing a bear pattern, like a rising wedge, head and shoulders top, double top or the like, from which a downside break has taken place on volume. If you don't yet know what these patterns are, ask someone who does. Or read the books on charting recommended in the Resources chapter of this book.

THE ALL-IMPORTANT TREND LINE

We'll assume you took a position and are now short. At this point, you should place a stop-loss order the same day. Day traders use day orders (to expire at the close of the same market day). But most use GTC (good till canceled) or good till the end of the week or month. You may want to place the order about one or two points above the downtrend line so that when the stock breaks its downtrend you want out of your short at once, not caring if it's a so-called false break or a genuine reversal. If you do that, make it a stop-close-only order, so you don't get stopped out on a fluke intra-day spurt. Basis the close is safer.

CHANGE STOP

One key to the success of the plan is to change the stop-loss order as needed, based on the new level of the trend line, which is never the same two days in a row in any stock with a steep trend line, and based on the stock price change. Hopefully the price drops, if so you'll place your stop-loss order a bit lower than the prior level. Keep repeating this process as necessary, whether for days, weeks, months, or years. If the price stands *still* but the trend line angle makes the last stop look too high or low, change the stop.

Thus, you seal in your profit. It never gets away from you. A loss never takes place unless it occurs in the first few days after you take a position, in which case you are out quickly and with a minimum loss, so you can try another. You can't be right in stock selection more than perhaps 6, 7, or maybe 8 times in 10. Even if you are right only 4 or 5 times, but on those occasions let your profits mount, you should still come out ahead.

NO METHOD PERFECT

There will be cases where your stock hits its stop-loss order and then reverses. That can't be helped. You bought insurance against bigger losses with your stop and you must be content with that knowledge.

If you start your action under this formula very late in a movement, you'll find you get stopped out rather soon in most of your picks.

This can't be helped either. But, when you see it happening, step out awhile to see if the trend is not indeed slowly changing, in which case you'll now want to begin using the same method on the long side, buying stocks instead of shorting.

ONE STOCK ONLY

The best way to begin using this method is to use it for a single stock at a time. It's extremely difficult for most people to watch two or three positions at the same time successfully. Unless you're one of those rare people who can literally do two things at once, stay away from two or more positions when you first follow this formula. One stock gives you the advantage of total concentration. If you wish to increase your investment, do it in the same stock, adding to your holding, but only as it moves favorably for you.

ODD LOTS VERSUS ROUND LOTS

To maximize profits, try to deal only in round lots (100 shares) even though it may mean you have to deal in cheaper stocks.

The fraction of a point lost in buying and reselling an odd lot (under 100 shares) forces you to be that bit more right and cuts into your profit or makes the loss larger.

DON'T TRY TO OUTGUESS THE MARKET

Under this approach, you never try to anticipate what the market or your stock is going to do next. You act as though you didn't care. You just keep moving that stop each day or so, and nothing else interests you. You need not decide to sell out or cover. You just allow yourself to be stopped out. The only partial exception to this is, as mentioned before, when your studies show a reversal is taking place in the market averages. Then, you may wish to bring your stop orders (up or down) very close, so that the slightest move of your stock against you takes you out.

MORE ON STOCK SELECTION

When you are using this formula, there are a few extra hints that may help in taking your initial position. Avoid taking a position if you are in grave doubt about the market as a whole.

Wait until you feel a trend is under way. This doesn't mean a trend is established so thoroughly that everyone can see it or so old that reversal is in the air. But it should be a "confirmed trend," as qualified by lower lows and lower highs in the DJIA (for short positions), or higher highs and higher lows (for long positions).

Usually avoid cheap stocks (stocks selling under $5). Favor stocks in new high ground for the year if going long, or new low ground if going short. Favor stocks with relatively few shares *only* if the short interest in the stock is not unfavorable to your position. Favor stocks with a big short interest as compared to total shares out if buying long, or a small short interest if selling short.

STOCK SHORT INTEREST RATIO

A long-time favorite indicator of mine is the individual stock short interest ratio. Here, you take the stock's total number of shares outstanding and subtract all the shares you know to be held by funds and institutions (this information is available in *Barron's, Standard & Poor's,* etc.). Then, divide the latest short interest figure in that stock (multiplied by 100) by the remaining shares outstanding.

For example, let's say you wish to calculate the ratio for ZIP Corp. It has 1,000,000 shares out. Institutions and funds hold 500,000. Maybe you learn also (from its S&P sheet) that the president and officers own 250,000 shares.

This leaves 250,000 rather freely floating so far as you can see. You look up the short interest in *Barron's* or the *Wall Street Journal* or elsewhere. It shows 60,000 shares short. You divide 6,000,000 (60,000 multiplied by 100) by 250,000. The answer shows a ratio of 24%, very high indeed and a good stock to buy long perhaps, but not one to short. The relationship between shorts and shares out is too high for a short, since the number of shorts to longs constitutes a quarter of the stock out. A short squeeze is highly probable in such a case.

If the ratio were as low as, say, 7%, you could consider the short interest as negligible, and freely short the stock in question. Although there is no guarantee of success simply because of its ratio, at least you are assured of avoiding a *trap*, and you take a position *with* the stock, not against it.

A DOUBLE-CHECK

An extra measure of safety can be added if you compare the weekly volume of trading for your stock (information available in *Barron's* or weekend newspapers) with the stock's short interest. As a loose rule of thumb, if the stock is trading less shares in a week than its short interest, the gearing is powerfully bullish.

Conversely, if the trading volume is, for example, 50,000 for the week's total and the short interest in the stock is only 9,000, then it's bearish. There is no technical support in the stock from its short interest in this example, and it's a suitable candidate for shorting consideration.

This double-check may, in a pinch, be used instead of the previously discussed short interest ratio, if you have difficulty getting the data.

CONSIDER THE INDUSTRY

This is also of importance and can add much to the strength of your position. By picking a stock that is part of an upward (or downward if you are shorting) moving group, you get the odds working for you to a considerably higher degree. Industries take turns at being in or out of fashion, usually based on earnings or prospects of earnings. But some stocks are difficult to place in an industry group. Others are in two groups at once.

Those who think industry groups are the most important selection factor often end up in the right group but pick the wrong stock. Thus, I feel that industry consciousness is only helpful if you select your stock by chart analysis.

LONG OR SHORT

I wish to emphasize again that this technique is equally applicable to buying stocks or selling them short. Some variations of this method are occasionally seen on the long side, but one rarely sees it done on the short side in bear markets. Yet you can see that the principle is the same for either type of market.

ATTITUDE IS VITAL

I would remind you again that your attitude is critical in making money, and, with this or any method, attitude will determine your degree of success. To make profits consistently, you must be more interested in making money and cutting losses short than in being right.

Newcomers may find this strange and many old-timers would be reluctant to admit it, but many people in the market subconsciously feel it's more important to be right than to make money. They think both are important. But pride is such an important factor that they refuse to admit mistakes (thus hanging on to falling stocks) and wait too long for the market to move around to prove their feeling about it was right.

To make money, you must have no pride of opinion. You must care only about making profits and not hesitate for one second to admit you made a mistake, and reverse your direction from forward to back or back to forward. By the way, it's easier to admit mistakes to yourself if you don't tell friends or family about your positions—as you hate to lose face in their eyes. So keep quiet!

SUMMARY—STICK TO YOUR RULES

To summarize this relatively safe trading method: Select a high volume stock with a sharp trend line. Stick to one stock. Stay in it until stopped out. And change stop-loss orders as necessary—based on the trend line and price. Trade short or long depending on the trend. When in doubt, stay out. Check the short interest. Forget pride of opinion.

I can think of no better incentive for you to set some kind of trading tactics or rules (such as those outlined in the next chapter) than to quote this: "A bookkeeper (in a brokerage office) kept 5,000 accounts, and he only knew of one man's account that showed a profit." This was written by E.E. Hooker, Jr in *You Can't Win in Wall Street*, 1927.

The odds are against the undisciplined in the stock market. If you, like me, can't leave it alone, then increasing your know-how is your only hope of gain and survival. You should run scared as a habit. But if you follow a sound set of rules, your tactics will be your salvation. The principal reason people lose money in the market is their lack of a full set of simple rules for every situation, or, more commonly, not following them. What do you hear more often in this business than someone saying, "I knew I should have sold it when it hit 125, but ..."

So, set some rules and stick with them.

15
Rules for Being a Flexible Investor

Largely because money moves across the world in the time it takes to strike a key on a computer, markets have become vastly more volatile and sensitive. Time-tested market tools and models that date back 60 years or more are still excellent indicators of market direction; but short to intermediate reactions in markets are ever more jittery, which pressure our tools. And when a default in an emerging nation can cause a major ripple in markets across the world, we must be a good deal more flexible in our investment strategies than in the past.

Also, in the last 10 years, the futures and derivatives markets have exploded, whereby the value of a derivative is linked to an underlying asset, but is several degrees more leveraged than a simple stock, bond, or commodity, bought on margin. All these factors require a level of flexibility of thinking that would have scared the investor of 40 years ago.

It requires what used to be called having a "trader's mentality" of the market. Although the phrase has a stronger application now. When we say a trader's frame of reference, we really mean being pliable, alert, and willing to get out of things quickly, and usually aiming at shorter-term profits. It's a concept that may be emotionally hard for many investors to grasp after the late 1990s' bubble, when buying almost anything and holding on to it was considered a brilliant "investment strategy."

But, even if we enter a new bull market in the near future, the era of being able to buy almost anything and expecting it to make you a profit without monitoring has vanished for at least the next decade.

The rules that follow are not just rules that apply to any new stock you are thinking of purchasing or selling short, but rules you should apply to every stock now in your portfolio each time you review it. Even those holdings that you hope will be ultra long term should be viewed as if you were about to buy them for the first time. Then, you will be in the right emotional frame of mind to get rid of underperformers and replace them with stocks more likely to do better.

1.   Almost nobody is a born trader. You have to learn. It's almost against human nature, because most of us are averse to change. But it can be learned, like any skill.

2.   In the current environment, there is no good alternative to trading. To "invest long term" works in some time frames. But this isn't one of them. The long-term philosophy is often unproductive because it means you sometimes will buy and hold, without stops, and the investment falls. You can incur major losses. Some hold losers hoping for recovery, which "if" they come back can take a long time, during which time you may need the money.

I am not suggesting you become a day trader. Merely that you watch your investments closely on a daily (if possible) or weekly basis, through the eyes of the market indicators in this book. And ask yourself, "If I didn't own this stock, would I buy it right now?" If the answer is, "No," then switch to a stock that will work harder for you.

Today, you can no longer afford to treat your stock portfolio as a bank account, as many did in the last decade of the 20th century. You've got to watch your portfolio with a trader's eye and perspective.

3.   There are times when buying a stock that's already high—on a chart breakout, out of a consolidation pattern—is proper. Likewise, there are times when buying a stock at a new low price is proper—if accompanied by a chart that reflects accumulation or the end of a downswing, as in a down wedge pattern. Frankly, without a chart, you are flying blind. Don't get greedy on rises. Start selling after very sharp upsweeps and keep moving stops up. When a stock turns negative on its chart, sell it, or sell it short.

4.   Hedging. This technique can be a godsend. It can prevent you from taking a loss. In theory, it works like this: Let's say you buy a stock with bullish fundamentals. But it starts down. Do you sell? If there's no chart sell signal and if you think the stock's fundamentals have not changed, you can hedge. You can't know how far this correction (if that's what it

is) will last, and almost nobody can (or should) afford to sit just holding a stock as it slides. Instead, you can hedge, which means you go short while holding the stock long. Then, when the price falls to an area of support and begins to stabilize, you cover your short at a profit and wait till the price rise finally gets back to your purchase price and then, hopefully, into a profit. Thus, by hedging, you have avoided a loss and probably ended up with two profits.

In some cases, you may not get out with two profits: but only one and a smaller loss in the second position than if you hadn't hedged at all. Either way, you salvaged the situation through defensive action. Some people hedge at the start, go long and short the same day and then drop one when a trend is clear. It's insurance trading.

5.   Learn at least *something* about charts. Preferably learn a *lot*. And, if you can spare the time, make your own charts, because by doing so you get a feel for the "personality" of a stock, and which chart patterns work for it and which don't. You can't really make quality investment decisions, in my opinion, without charts. It's possible to chart *every* kind of market.

As I said before, if you can spare the time, don't immediately rely on printed or Internet chart services to supply you with charts. For the first few months, do it yourself. When you have a "feel" for how charts work, you can save time by using chart services.

6.   You'll need to work out your own final strategy for some aspects of trading because we all have different temperaments, hang-ups, fears, levels of anxiety, risk-aversion levels, ego, needs, etc. Some are happiest and can function most efficiently always taking small profits, selling after their investment has made a single leg up. Others like to buy more as their stock rises, in hopes of a big harvest when it eventually turns down. Still others, while reexamining their portfolio on a weekly basis and asking themselves if they would buy any of their holdings if they didn't already own them, prefer to keep their initial positions without adding to them, as long as the stocks hold steady. There isn't room here for all possible approaches, but it's helpful to realize the need to formulate a trading strategy that suits your personality, makes you a happy camper.

7.   Amazingly, markets usually give you a second chance. If you miss the first chance to buy or sell, markets quite often give you a second opportunity. It may not be precisely at the same price, but there is normally a pull back (up or down) that lets you in. This helps you to both exit and acquire. Bear it in mind so you don't panic and sell too low or buy too high, like on an upside breakout. You can buy a bit after

the breakout, but then wait to buy more till you get a pullback followed by a slight move back up, to confirm that your original chart interpretation was correct. And the same in reverse when selling or shorting after a downside breakout.

8. The best answer to the question, "When do I sell?" is this: If the stock you buy falls immediately after purchase, you should sell at once (or hedge it with a short). But if the stock you buy rises, you have two choices: either sell when it reaches a target (predetermined by a chart pattern), or, if it fails to reach its target, sell when it falls and threatens your profit. Never let a profit disappear and turn into a loss (or bigger loss) if you can help it.

9. Get in the habit of blaming yourself if you lose money—not your broker, advisor, markets, etc. I find I can give identical advice to four people and three will profit and one will lose. Learning *how* to be a winner is the key. Ultimately, that key is not being right about the direction your stock will go, but having the right frame of mind to know when to sell, or hedge, and not place your ego above profits.

10. They used to say it's bad if you make money on your first stock purchase. It is still true. If you suddenly think you know how to play the game now and you can't go wrong, take care. That ego or pride-of-opinion factor can cause you to stumble. It is helpful to keep a list of market losses taped to your computer, with the date, amount lost, and why you believe the trade went wrong, to remind yourself of how easy it is to lose money if you allow your ego to get in the way, and/or don't follow the rules.

11. The final rule is to make up your own rules. You know best what you can live with. Study all the guidelines herein and then compose a list of your own that you think will work for you. Review it monthly for possible improvement, particularly if you lost money in the prior month. It can also help to make a happy list of winners with the reasons why. It can lead you to form a habit of only using certain techniques.

CONCLUSION

To evolve an investment strategy of buying and selling uniquely tailored to your personality will give you immense power, confidence (not arrogance), profits, and peace of mind.

Without a personal list of rules that become your strategy for investing and trading, you may learn how to predict the direction of the market with accuracy and still lose money because you didn't do something at the right time. Timing comes via your strategies—and can spell the difference between profits and losses.

16
Defensive Investments that Allow You to Sleep Nights

"Gentlemen prefer bonds."

Andrew Mellon, financier and secretary of the Treasury, 1921–1932

PERSONAL MEASURES YOU CAN TAKE

Every asset you have, needs to be reevaluated in a bear market. This is because bear markets "usually" (not always) are bellwether indicators of recessions or depressions.

Thus, not just your portfolio of stocks, but your real estate, deposited cash, business, government bonds, and other assets must be analyzed for safety. It may be that the "defensive" portion of your portfolio (non-stock holdings) simply needs to be increased. But, before you make a decision on how to change your portfolio, it is necessary to "Take a View," as outlined in Chapter 3.

You should examine political, economic, and monetary data to decide what *sort* of recession and/or bear market is likely to evolve over the next few months, or years:

- Will it be short and sharp à la 1987 or 1990, where the underlying economic and financial infrastructure won't be damaged very much if at all?
- Will it be an inflationary recession as we saw in the 1970s? A recession that may not be very deep, but will be protracted because it cannot end until inflation is squeezed out of the economy?

- Will it be deflationary, or just disinflationary? No matter what government does to create liquidity, if it is countered by businesses and consumers who spend less in an anxiety-ridden environment, government efforts will fail. For example, in the mid to late 1930s, in spite of Keynesian deficit spending, consumers were so worn down that nothing government did, stimulated the economy much, until war changed the mood of the consumer.
- Or will it be a combination of the above? Once you have made this assessment, you are ready to make changes to your portfolio.

In Chapter 12, I explained how John Templeton structures his portfolio in bull and bear markets. It is worth repeating here.

No matter what the investment or economic climate is, he mentally divides his portfolio in half, with 50% in long-term stock investments and the rest sometimes in stocks, sometimes in bonds, and sometimes in other defensive positions.

That is a very sound principle, though the 50% rule would have to be adjusted depending on your level of overall wealth. The value of the stock part of your portfolio should never be more than three times what you can afford to lose and still maintain your lifestyle. Put another way, any security in this part of your portfolio could fall 30% before you decide to cut your losses, or maybe decide to ride out the storm no matter how long that storm is, without threatening your ability to fund your children's college or your living standard during retirement.

During a bull market, such as we saw in the 1990s, it is likely you had a far greater portion of your assets in stocks. But, following Templeton's rule, even if you were 90% invested in stocks, you should have labeled 40% of those investments as "short term," needing to be monitored daily, or at least three times weekly. And you should have been ready to move out of them via stops and into bonds or other cash-equivalent investments as soon as it became clear the market was in a "bubble" phase. It was no secret.

This division of assets applies in bear markets as well, except what constitutes a defensive investment in a bear market depends on whether it is an inflationary or deflationary bear market.

If you decide the bear market is going to be similar to 1987 or 1990, there is little you need to do except sell those stocks that are unlikely to participate in a new recovery. The rest of this chapter will deal with more retracted bear markets.

BONDS AND CASH-EQUIVALENT INVESTMENTS

Unless you believe that inflation will rapidly increase to 5% or more, having a major portion of your portfolio in bonds and bank accounts at interest is prudent. If bank interest rates are too low (e.g., 2%), you can substitute quality corporate bonds. Treasury or other government bonds with a 5–10 year maturity are the safest, because no matter how bad things get, it is unlikely that any government in the industrialized world will default on their bonds. In addition, in many countries there is a tax break on government (national, state, or local) bonds, which makes the real rate of interest higher than the actual rate.

In an inflationary environment, bonds still have their place. During the 1970s, for example, while the dollar was suffering from high inflation, the Swiss franc and the German mark were not. Many Americans chose to put money into Swiss and German bonds and bank accounts at interest, and made considerable profits. It was, in fact, advice I gave my newsletter readers at the time!

REAL ESTATE

Unless high inflation occurs in a recession, investment real estate should be liquidated or cut back. The odds say it will not rise in value; thus, you risk it either going down or, at best, standing still. In a deflationary recession, if you hold rental property, the odds are high that rents will decline, and, if you want to sell the property later, there will be a dearth of buyers.

Once you are satisfied that a protracted bear market exists on Wall Street, you must assume a business recession or depression will occur. With a business depression comes lack of spare cash by potential buyers of your real estate, so it's better to get out before this happens—at least real estate other than your residence. Most people want to keep their home for emotional reasons, regardless of how it fares as an investment. However, if we are headed for a depression and you aren't "married" to your home, you could sell before property falls much. Also, it will be cheaper to rent than to own.

In a deflationary recession, interest rates usually decline, so try to refinance any real estate you plan to hold at lower mortgage rates. Of course, by the time you make a decision to sell—if you do—prices will have dropped and real estate will be harder to sell. It's the same with stock values. But the loss of a *top* price, and perhaps a later actual loss from cost, is still better than risking holding property as it goes ever lower as the worst of a recession or depression bites. Moreover, your cash from a sale could be earning interest or be invested elsewhere.

The worst that can happen after you sell real estate is that a business recession will not be very deep or that it will be short-lived. It's the same risk as when you sell a falling stock only to see it rise again. Nothing is certain. But the more you study markets, the better your decisions.

But, if the rate of inflation suddenly speeds up while business is slowing down, real estate will become a way to preserve value. In an inflationary bear market, real estate is a major defensive investment. Don't sell.

ARE BANKS SAFE IN A MAJOR BEAR MARKET?

In 1929, the banks held gloriously for a number of months and everyone was proud of them. In November 1930 (a year after the crash), the *Literary Digest* said, "There have been no important banking failures as a result of the shakeup, attesting to the strength of the banking system in the USA." But a year later, on December 5, 1931, they ran an editorial on what a good sign it was that "banking failures were declining." Bank failures were down from 166 a week to 18 a week!

It is true that many safeguards have been built into the system that were not there in 1929. And if the US banking system was insulated from the rest of the world, it's possible there would be few banking problems. But we live in an interdependent world.

As of 2002, we're in a major global recession. The world's banking system is only as strong as its weakest link(s). It is possible that there would not have been a banking crisis in the US in 1930 if a major Austrian bank, the Credit Anstalt, had not collapsed, which caused a ripple effect across a depressed Europe and the US. It is probable that, if the Austrian recession had been an isolated event and the rest of Europe and the US had enjoyed 1990s-type prosperity, the collapse of a minor European bank would not have become the straw that broke the back of European and US banking. The Asian banking crisis, which hit its peak in 1997, did not affect the rest of the world because Europe and the US were still enjoying unprecedented prosperity, and so were in a position, via the IMF, to support the shaky banking and finance systems in most of South-East Asia.

Should a similar crisis occur in 2002, 2003, or 2004, with the world already in the throes of a recession, what was able to be isolated in 1997 could easily become the Credit Anstalt of the future just ahead. Let me hasten to add that, as of this writing, there is no rumor of any major bank in the US or Europe failing. But things change. Monitor the situation regularly, to make sure that a financial crisis somewhere else in the world doesn't escalate at a time when the West doesn't have the resources to contain its effects. Read an international newspaper daily for straws in the wind. You won't see them on TV!

IF YOU OWN YOUR OWN BUSINESS

What should the little or big businessman do about his business in a really bad *deflationary* bear market and recession? Big business just has to take it on the chin. They will do what they must do. They will slash payrolls, cut costs in every way, as they have been doing in 2000 and 2001. Small businesses can consider selling out, if they can find a buyer. It depends on whether they feel they can survive in an economic climate where they may lose, say, 30 to 40% of their gross income. If they can cut costs and still make a bare living, then they too can hang on, along with General Motors (whose car sales could fall to a trickle).

Medium-sized businesses will probably gravitate toward mergers and down-sizing to save overheads. This will result in fewer jobs, but many businesses will be saved.

In an *inflationary* recession, owning your own business becomes a defensive investment. Your plant and equipment are "tangible investments" whose value increases as the currency depreciates. Generally, during inflationary times, consumer confidence remains high. So, though you may make less "real" profit (adjusted) in an inflationary recession than you would in low-inflation boom times, your business becomes a major defensive investment.

TANGIBLE ASSETS

In an *inflationary* recession, if you own a stamp or coin collection of value, jewelry, rare stones, antiques art, old cars, or a warehouse full of merchandise, hang on. Their value is likely to increase much more than the increase in inflation. But if the recession is *deflationary*, all the above would decrease in value. If the recession becomes a depression, probably *much* less. So, buy and sell accordingly.

GOLD

In times of uncertainty, gold bullion, gold mining shares, and gold coins rise in price. This is true whether the climate is deflationary or inflationary, though gold usually rises more during times of inflation than deflation. To those who claim that gold as a store of value is passé, I would point out that a large percentage of the world's banking reserves is still held in gold. And hundreds of millions of people in Asia and the Middle East buy gold daily as their safe haven. Gold demand has exceeded supply for several years. A bull market in gold technically began in November 2000. For the year 2001, gold mining shares outperformed all stock averages.

Every portfolio should have a survival gold holding. In an inflationary recession, gold becomes a *major* investment. In a deflationary recession, if the anxiety factor is high enough, gold is still attractive as an investment. But gold does not follow "normal" investment rules.

During the 1930s, US gold ownership was forbidden, which enabled Roosevelt to raise the price of gold by government decree. It is significant that in a deflationary environment, even before the price of gold was officially raised, gold mining shares rose, and dramatically so during the depression. And, though Roosevelt decided on a new price for gold, it is significant that he raised the price almost 60%, from $20.67 to $35 an ounce—a price that remained until the early 1970s. In the view of this author, another 60% rise could occur soon, but via the free market. This suggests that, even in a deflationary recession, gold is a good investment. During the inflationary 1970s, gold went from $35 to a record high of $850 an ounce on January 21, 1980. But gold is not an investment one only buys and holds, not even in a bear market. It's more of a buy, sell on run-ups, buy on sharp declines. Sell again. Buy again (while keeping a core holding).

The reason is that governments recognize that gold stands, to a large extent, as *judge and jury* on their actions. Therefore, several governments (e.g., US and the UK) do whatever they can to keep the price of gold down. In the 1970s, during the first inflationary surge in 1974, government was able to talk the gold price down, while they dealt with inflation. Their continued propaganda campaign against gold was so successful that it was not until 1978, when it was clear to all that inflation was not going to be controlled, that the gold price exploded. Those who bought gold when it was $35 an ounce and sold it at around $800 an ounce made huge profits. I urged my readers to buy in this period. But it was not the sort of investment that just climbed a trend line calmly. Gold behaves more like a pressure cooker than a stock. When it begins to rise, governments do whatever they can to depress the price. Only when all their best efforts fail does gold rise to its true free-market price.

There is strong circumstantial evidence that, for the last 12 years, the price of gold has been deliberately depressed via sales and hedging operations. Be that as it may, what is clear is that when economic conditions or the stock market get really bad, and the gold price begins to rise appreciably, certain governments do and will do all they can to hold the price down as long as they can. Greenspan said so before Congress. It also happened in the days of the London Gold Pool in the 1960s.

Therefore, in the early stages of a bear market, whether it is inflationary or deflationary, I suggest a 10–15% investment in gold bars, gold bullion coins, *and* gold mining shares—all three. You can then add to your bullion and share holdings by increments, as the bear and gold markets evolve.

CONCLUSION

This book is designed to cover all types of bear markets. About half of them in our history have not been severe enough to require all the alternative actions listed herein. Each bear market must be judged on its own demerits. Their severity is never the same twice in a row.

But an assessment of any bull or bear market is an evolving perspective. Learn to reexamine your perspectives on a regular basis, and ask yourself the hard questions as to whether your prior opinion, based on the new evidence, still applies. You can get help from quality investment letters, but not from TV or stockbrokers, due to their vested interest in bullishness.

THE MARKET IS FOR EVERYONE

The principles outlined in this chapter are the same for the man with $30,000 as for the man with three hundred million dollars. The same is true of all parts of this book. During the glory days of the late 1990s, most small investors saw the stock market as little more than a bank, and gains as simply a higher "interest" than their regular bank could offer. I remember seeing an investment club organizer interviewed on TV. He announced, with a perfectly straight face, that they were conservative, that they did not speculate in leading-edge technology firms even though potentially higher profits could be made. They were content and expected to make 20% per year, no more! Every year. Like an entitlement.

The uniqueness of the dot com era is summed up in the assumption that the expectation of a guaranteed 20% profit per year was *conservative*! Most expected 30–35%.

Even if the bear market and recession at hand end without a crash scene, we are never likely to see a market like the late 1990s again in our lifetimes. Henceforth, everybody, no matter how little money they have to invest, will need to be responsible for their own financial future, without help from a no-brainer bull market. And that takes work. All the work explained in this book, and beyond.

DOING NOTHING IS STILL A DECISION

Even if you decide to "do nothing" with your money, or want to get out of the market and park your money in government bonds or hide it under the mattress, the act of deciding to do nothing is an investment decision. You take a stand regardless of how you hold your assets. If you elect to leave them where they are, because you don't really know what to do, you have made a decision for which you *should have* weighed the evidence.

There are people who were aware, as early as mid-2000, that markets were heading lower, but who allowed their stocks to lose even more value because they were not able to look reality in the face, take responsibility for their own financial future, and make portfolio adjustments based on the new conditions. After years of huge profits, though logically it appeared that era was over, emotionally many investors were not willing to accept the fact.

Many of those same people are now saying it is "too late to sell." If they are convinced, based on their best analysis and judgment, that the bear market of 2001–2002 will be so short and shallow that it really is too late to sell, then good luck to them. I am merely saying that it's dangerous to base investment decisions on what you think/hope will happen and using data selectively to support a refusal to change course.

"It is never too late to do the right thing" based on your best judgment, which you arrived at after doing the necessary study to form your conclusions. If you are wrong in selling, you can always buy back. But, if you ignore the signals, you can't go back to those higher prices and do it over differently.

My suggestion, overall, is to do a bit of several things in case, even after you have worked hard to come to the right conclusion, you are wrong in your interpretations. Never be too radical in your solutions.

The world, owing to ever more instant communications, moves faster. Some factors that affect longer-term trends can change overnight. But, overall, longer-term trends still evolve slowly. So, provided you stay alert, there is usually time to adjust your strategies to changing events. But spread your risks, and make haste in increments. Incorporate new information into your long-term view, and modify it and your portfolio mix accordingly. Those are the ingredients of defensive investing.

Part VI
THE EMOTIONAL ASPECT

"Manias, panics, and crashes are the consequence of an economic environment that cultivates cupidity, chicanery, and rapaciousness rather than a devout belief in the Golden Rule."

Peter L. Bernstein in his Foreword to *Manias, Panics, and Crashes*, by Charles P. Kindleberger, John Wiley & Sons, Inc., 2000

17
Human Psychology in the Marketplace

"There are no certainties in this investment world, and where there are no certainties, you should begin by understanding yourself."

James L. Fraser

This is perhaps the hardest chapter to write and that probably means it's the most important. A writer friend once told me, as we exchanged experiences over a good dinner and a bottle of "bull's blood" wine, in London, that from his writing experience, the things that write easily are usually the worst and least useful. The logic of this is that what flows easily is no doubt loaded with preconceived notions, predigested thinking, and very little new, deep, penetrating analysis.

I inserted that lengthy preamble to impress on you the importance of this chapter. For, although emotions seem to have little bearing on getting more market know-how, they are on the other hand the single factor most likely to keep you from *using* the know-how you accumulate, or using it correctly, or at the right time.

EMOTION SPELLS TROUBLE

Our emotions are our enemies in the stock market and in business generally. In bull markets, we become ebullient and tend to buy, buy, buy, almost blindly. We hear only what we want to hear. We want prices to rise so we act like a bull. This lays us wide open for the kill.

Conversely, at the end of a bear market, fear, doubt, and lack of confidence grow until we are blind to the market's signals that a new bull market is beginning.

But these are the extremes, the top and bottom. Most of the time is spent well within those limits. And, here, our optimistic nature does us great damage in a bear market, which is our primary concern in this book. As optimists, it's awkward for us to try to make money by shorting stocks, hoping stocks will fall. A short sale seems risky since it is contrary to our nature.

To profit from a bear market requires that to some degree we suspend our need for bullish hope over the short and medium term, and concentrate instead on expectations for a falling market. This goes against human nature, and when things look to become worse than they have been in the past, or the future looks, at best, ambiguous, we tend to assume the *worst* possible outcome is the only one. Though history proves that, over thousands of years, there have been very few apocalyptic times, we have a hard time investing with a downtrend, while judging that move as only temporary.

The truth is that a short sale in a bear market is likely to make you more money, faster, than a stock bought long in a bull market. This is because the pull of a bear market is shorter term and propelled by fear—thus, usually stronger. Because it is against our very nature, we will be constantly vigilant for signs of a reversal back to more comfortable optimism, so we are more likely to complete a bear market short sale at the correct time than we are to sell a stock at the top of a bull market.

FEAR AND ITS CURE

Fear is the most powerful emotion we have in bear markets, and probably in life generally. If we put fear under the microscope, we find it is usually based on the *ambiguity* of a situation rather than on a known bad outcome. We fear what we don't know, so we exaggerate the possible ramifications. It is therefore emotionally easier to deny the existence of a bear market for as long as possible in hopes that it will go away and you don't have to deal with it. Unfortunately, that approach is the sure road to shrinking assets.

The cure: increasing our knowledge in these areas where it's needed. Step up our knowledge of bear markets, depressions, recessions, and the tactics needed to profit from these situations. As we do this, our fear will diminish, though it may never totally disappear.

It may give you courage to know that the biggest fortunes of all recorded history were often made when things were at their worst.

Someone recently said courage is a vital need in the market. To be a really successful investor, you must have extraordinary courage. You will be fully invested when the majority are afraid to venture. You will be in cash when most are still buying their heads off.

Bear markets seem to require an extra measure of courage.

Rothschild once advised, "Buy when the blood is running in the streets." He said it all. I can only expand on this theme. In the 1929 crash, several millionaires were made, not because they had big fortunes to do it with, but because they had big know-how.

THEORY VERSUS REALITY

You can have a system or an approach to market investment that works beautifully on paper but falls apart in practice. Why? Because, when it comes to turning decisions into actions, the emotions dictate part of the answer. When it's real money, the decisions are harder, the heart beats faster, and our fears or euphoria come boiling to the surface.

What's needed is realism and just plain common sense. But that's an easily spoken mouthful of words, and damnably hard to practice.

DANGERS OF EMOTIONAL DECISIONS

The French sociologist Gustave LeBon wrote 100 years ago:

> "The crowd has never thirsted for the truth. It turns aside from evidence that is not to its taste, preferring to glorify and follow error, if the way of error appears attractive enough, and seduces them. Whoever can supply the crowd with attractive emotional illusions may easily become their master, and whoever attempts to destroy such firmly entrenched illusions of the crowd is almost sure to be rejected."

However, there is hope. There is one way the masses can be convinced of the truth. Naturally, it's belated. LeBon put it this way:

> "An often repeated reference to past experience is almost the only effective process by which a truth may be firmly established in the thinking of the masses. Thus, false illusions that have grown dangerously large for the public's own good may eventually be destroyed. To this end, however, the truth as illustrated by past experience must be brought forward in various manners on a large scale, and this process should be repeated frequently and emphatically."

When we read things like this, we like to think they are talking about all *other* people. We think that "the public" never includes us. But in fact it does.

NO EXCEPTIONS

Emotions are the common denominator that makes us all the same, and they can bring down the mightiest. Emotions have separated a king from his throne more than once. The examples are endless. They provide that, unless we can control our emotions or have some· measure of control, *they* control us. Emotionally-backed decisions (especially in the stock market) are invariably bad ones, if emotion is largely what supports them.

BE CONTRARY

One of the reasons our emotions get us into trouble in the stock market is that the essence of being human is the need to belong, to be "part of the group," and it's easy to be swept up in a wave of either euphoria or pessimism. Again, knowledge is our best defense. In my chapter on contrary thinking (Chapter 18), you will see that the best vaccination you can give your brain is to reject *everything* automatically. Then, after rejecting it, you can study it and see if it merits accepting. This "cooled off" method of thinking will enable you to control your emotions to a large degree.

FULL CONTROL UNLIKELY AND POSSIBLY EVEN UNDESIRABLE

Mind you, complete emotional control is probably impossible. But if you simply step up your thinking and control processes, you'll be ahead of the crowd. And when you fall short, take comfort in the fact that the really huge fortunes made on Wall Street, particularly during times of financial distress, were made in the main by people who lacked the normal social bonds to friends and family most of the rest of us need to be happy. I am not even suggesting that you strive to acquire this level of control. Merely that you never lose sight of what your basic common sense is saying, no matter how euphoric or depressed the mood of your fellow investors becomes.

STUDY OF CROWDS

If you study the psychology of crowds (there are several books on the subject: e.g., *The Crowd* by Gustave LeBon and *Extraordinary Popular Delusions and the Madness of Crowds* by Charles MacKay, both classics), you will see how people's behavior, like most things in life, tends to go from one extreme to another. People become irrationally bullish or bearish, which is why price swings go to extremes.

KNOWLEDGE AIDS OBJECTIVITY

All knowledge is useful in the stock market. It is made up of the thinking and emotions of people everywhere and is under the domination of the sequential influence of cause and effect. The more you know about people, about human behavior, about business, about market, economic, and social history, the better able you are to cope with today's market.

Much of what we do by way of evaluation and decision making comes from processing the present in the light of past experience, either what we have read about or have personally experienced. This often happens subconsciously. So the more you know, the more realistic will be your market judgment.

MOST BELIEVE THEMSELVES OBJECTIVE

Most people believe themselves to be clear, calm, unemotional thinkers who reasonably weigh all the facts. Most of us, however, are either unwilling or unable to analyze ourselves accurately and objectively enough to be a lasting success in the stock market.

However, there is a twist here. Women are generally regarded as the more emotional sex. Yet, I know a number of couples where the man has too much ego invested in the prior buy decision to sell when the time is right. But the wife does not. In one case, they deliberately set their account up in different names so that when the time is right to sell, and the man is emotionally unable to execute the trade, his wife does it and tells him about it only after it is a *fait accompli*.

Perhaps, on a deep level, women have a greater sense of survival than men because, ever since cave-dwelling days, the ultimate responsibility for the family has fallen on the woman. Hence, while men have this battle between survival and ego, women have no such conflict. My experience has shown that those who do achieve some measure of objectivity and emotional control readily admit they have a problem and that it is hard to beat.

It's like knowledge. Those who think they know all the answers, in reality, often know very little. Those who know a great deal feel they know hardly anything. The more you learn, the more you find there is to learn and the less arrogant you are about what you think you know. There seems to be a measurable emotional sequence. In order: fear, pessimism, despair, caution, desire, confidence, faith, hope, enthusiasm, optimism, exuberance, and greed.

But none of what I have said so far means you should *try* to react unemotionally. That's impossible. But you can examine all the evidence you have, and then have a conversation with yourself, as a sort of devil's advocate, alter ego, to convince yourself why your first emotional reaction was wrong. If you act on emotion and don't dampen it with factual reasoning, you are likely to make bad investment decisions.

EMOTIONAL CONTROL

If, to get a broader viewpoint, you study every available market approach and every technique, plus give yourself a good background knowledge of history, you will find that your emotions become more stable and manageable as your expertise and knowledge expand.

INTUITION AS A MARKET TOOL

Human judgment is at its best when it is based on reasoned conclusions that are the result of massive research, but tempered with intuition, which when used properly is an emotional *gut feel* based on complex patterns of knowing, where we are not conscious of how we arrive at this (usually emotional) conclusion. We all know more than we think we do. As we go about our daily lives, our brain receives information that we are often not aware of. We sometimes dislike people when we first meet them. If we are decent human beings, we will dismiss that gut feel as irrational, and go out of our way to find their good points. Yet, more often than not, our first impression is the right one. Somehow, the complex signals of facial and body language told our subconscious minds things about that person that we did not know consciously. How many times have you heard the story that even though it took many months to formally decide to marry, within the *first hour* of a couple's first meeting, one or both of them knew they had found the person they wanted to marry?

Studies have been done of what makes a successful business leader. And, time and again, it is discovered that the truly brilliant business executives trust their intuition as much as their reason when making major decisions. It is said that Einstein would intuit his theories and then go back and find the mathematical grounds for *why* they were true.

But intuition, though apparently emotionally based, is very different from using emotional wish fulfillment as the basis for investment decisions.

We all know a lot more than we are conscious that we know. And the more we consciously learn by research or experience in any given field of endeavor, the more we should trust our intuition when making decisions.

It is for this reason that in earlier chapters I advise that you manually create your own charts for at least a few months, before you rely on an online service to provide them for you. Doing them manually will help develop a feel for the markets in ways that simply accepting ready-made charts will never do. But, though I advise you to cultivate stock-market intuition, I also warn you to be ever aware of the difference between a genuine gut feel for the near future, and an emotional *desire* for that feeling to be true.

ECONOMISTS USE PSYCHOLOGY TO PREDICT ECONOMICS

In recent years, a trend among economists is to consider social, political, and cultural factors as predictors of future economic growth or contraction. Perhaps the first advocate of this was Nobel Laureate F.A. Hayek, who began his career as an economist but very quickly turned to *sociology* and *philosophy* for answers as to why some countries are successful and some are not. In 1944, his book, *The Road to Serfdom*, was published in London. It explained partly in economic and partly in political and philosophical terms why communism doesn't work. It had limited success. As late as the 1960s, economic departments both in the US and in Europe had a problem with his holistic approach to the study of economics. But times have changed.

In 1997, Nobel Laureate Gary S. Becker, in *The Economics of Life*, addressed how social and political issues influence economic decisions. The following year, Harvard economics professor David S. Landes, in his book *The Wealth and Poverty of Nations*, drew the conclusion that the difference between success and failure depends on political and social belief systems that cultivate the values of "work, thrift, honesty, patience, tenacity." That: "If we learn anything from the history of economic development, it is that culture makes all the difference."

Robert William Fogel, Nobel Prize winner in 1993, takes holistic economics even further in his 2000 book, *The Fourth Great Awakening and the Future of Egalitarianism*, arguing that America is in the midst of a new wave of religious renewal, which will have profound and positive economic effects.

None of these books will tell you how to channel your emotions in a positive way in order to make profits in the stock market. However, they do demonstrate that the study of economics, and by association the stock market, is no longer regarded as only an inductive science. But, because economic activity is a deeply human activity, it is only by studying humanity in its *wholeness*, complete with its emotions and its political and religious beliefs, that we can make sensible decisions about what the future will look like, and what stocks to buy and sell. In short, the way to deal with emotions is to factor them into your investment decisions, to channel them in a positive way, instead of pretending they do not exist. And, most of all, know yourself and how your emotions affect the decisions that you make.

SPECIAL CAVEAT

If you have a big, personal, emotional problem such as divorce, separation, litigation, you will be wise if you get out of the market completely until your problem is resolved.

HELPFUL HINTS

1.   The stock market is the most difficult (as well as the most interesting) place of all places in which to make money. When you increase this difficulty by letting emotions dictate decisions, you make the odds insurmountable.

It may be oversimplification, but it is largely true that if a person is well adjusted with a good connection to friends and family, he or she can make a good emotional adjustment in the market. If he or she has a number of personal emotional problems, then it will be more difficult for him or her. So, make sure you know yourself, your limitations, your risk tolerance, etc.

2.   Research, read, and then read some more. Expose yourself only to the best-quality advisory services. Study all history, not just market history. Take time off to relax and be with your family. Associate with successful investors (they will be the ones who don't, as a rule, claim to be). And learn to think contrary.

"Rather we should say that the market is a voting machine, whereon countless individuals register choices which are the product partly of reason and partly of emotion."

Benjamin Graham and David Dodd

18
Contrary Opinion

"Mobs in their emotions are much like children, subject to the same tantrums and fits of fury."

Euripides (408 BC)

A skeptical attitude is vital. It is the underlying concept that can help us think straight and use "common sense," perspectives of what the pundits are saying. As corporate concentration in the media increases, the *diversity* of ideas and opinions expressed in newspapers, magazines, or on TV becomes less every day. Therefore, the ability to think contrary is much more important today than it was when I wrote my first book on bear markets nearly 40 years ago. The need to think contrary has increased *exponentially* in the last 10 years of mass mind murder by the media.

It's difficult to define contrary opinion. It isn't simply the contradiction of every opinion encountered. Neither is it safe to assume that the majority are wrong all the time. They are most likely to be wrong when there appears to be no division of opinion, and particularly at major turning points in stock market action.

The best definition of contrary opinion I have seen was in an article published in *Barron's* in September 1987. In it John Schultz wrote:

> "The guiding light of investment contrarianism is not that the majority view—the conventional, or received wisdom—is always wrong. Rather, it's that majority opinion tends to solidify into a dogma while its basic premises begin to lose their original validity and so become progressively more mis-priced in the marketplace."

We saw this "dogma" principle in action soon after George W. Bush was elected. After 8 years of a Clinton White House assuring the public that they had found the key to permanent prosperity, George Bush was soundly condemned for suggesting there were some weaknesses in the economy, in the belief that saying it would make it so. In a more rational time, the public would have been pleased that weaknesses had been pointed out in order to prevent them getting worse, or at least prepare for them. But in 2000 nobody wanted to listen.

The logic behind contrary opinion is that life is an ever-changing, highly complex, and dynamic process. An opinion or perspective that is totally sound at one point in time becomes outdated, so that by the time everybody has come around to believing it the set of circumstances that originally gave rise to that opinion have changed.

Also, mass thinking is always tinged with exaggeration, and tends to become extremist (dogmatic) thinking. This suggests a reaction to that concept is close at hand, to erase the extreme and restore balance.

STOCK MARKET APPLICATION

There is within all markets a group of savvy, experienced traders and investors who see buying (or selling) opportunities first, and they act. Soon, others see stocks beginning to move, although they don't necessarily know why stocks are moving, because the good economic news that drives stocks has not yet shown up in the published data. But, "it feels right," so they will buy to get in on the action. Gradually, more and more people see what is happening and, probably by this time, the reasons for the move are known (e.g., higher earnings or a drop in unemployment).

Eventually, a majority has been convinced that a major bull or bear market is under way and climbs aboard. It is at this point that the experienced traders decide that, as they have profits and the bandwagon is getting crowded, they will get out. And/or maybe even a bit of bad news has leaked out to those in the know.

Soon, others follow and so the trend reverses. This creates a continual flow of people opinions, first in one direction then another. Obviously, those who act first make the most money. The art of applying contrary opinion to the market, therefore, is to gauge at what point the technical and fundamental reasons are so obvious that they can be seen by anybody. That is the point at which the most skilled take their profits, and so should you.

Although this theory is known as thinking contra, this is not strictly true. What one aims at is, rather, to think before the crowd, and this is usually synonymous with thinking contra.

"But," you ask, "hasn't the age of instant communications destroyed this ebb and flow in markets?"

My answer: The *reverse* is true. During the buying frenzy in 1998 and 1999, insiders in Silicon Valley were warning that many of the high-tech start-ups were based on unsound business principles and, though their young CEOs became billionaires overnight, most of those who bought stocks in these companies would be left holding the bag.

But the voices of sanity were drowned out by the irresponsible TV financial news networks, who told ordinary investors what they wanted to hear. That is, that markets would go on rising, that the "new economy" had superseded the "old economy," and that none of the former rules by which one judged the economic health of a company were valid any more.

Modern communications make the extremes of euphoria and panic *greater* than they were even 20 years ago. Euphoria travels fast and furiously.

HISTORICAL EXAMPLES OF CONTRARY THINKING

There are great names in history who wrote about this approach:

- Goethe, the poet-philosopher, "I find more and more that it is well to be on the side of the minority, since it is always the more intelligent."
- Walter Lippmann, "Where all think alike, no one thinks very much."
- Jean Jacques Rousseau, "Follow the course opposite to custom and you will almost always do well."
- William Stanley Jevons, "As a general rule, it is foolish to do just what other people are doing, because there are almost sure to be too many people doing the same thing."
- Sir Francis Bacon, "Doubt all before you believe anything! Watch your idols!"

The majority were certainly wrong in the stock market in the late 1920s. Babson in 1927 wrote that 98% came out of the market poorer than they went in. And the crash that really wiped out fortunes was still 2 years away!

APPLY CONTRARY OPINION EVERYWHERE

You can best apply contrary opinion in the stock market if you form the *habit* of applying it in every area of human activity. The imminence of an event such as war and perhaps future acts of terrorism of the magnitude of September 11, 2001 are good examples.

Though I may live to eat these words, logically it would seem that no matter how big and well organized the global terrorist network is, one large reason

September 11 was possible was because nobody was prepared for it. It is fairly safe to say that, even if bin Laden and his cohorts had the same hatred for Europe as they apparently do for America, the hijacking of several passenger aircraft to be used as megaton bombs would have been far more difficult in Europe because Europe has had over 30 years' experience with dealing with terrorist groups of one sort or another.

If the US had had the same level of airport security and police awareness that Europe has had for decades, it is possible, even probable, that the hijackers would have been apprehended before they even got on the planes.

Yet, Americans are far more fearful today than they were prior to September 11, instead of feeling safer that counter-terrorism measures are being taken. That's because the panic/fear Americans feel is social, more than economic.

Y2K was another example, when many expected our computerized society to freeze up from a combination of outdated computer programs and hackers taking advantage of a weakness in the system to make matters worse. It didn't happen, not because there wasn't a problem, but because the problem was identified well in advance of the event, and dealt with. And security was beefed up so that would-be terrorist hackers had no window of opportunity to act.

Let's go back a few decades. For many years at the height of the Cold War, we lived in fear of an unprovoked Soviet nuclear attack, and some built fall-out shelters expecting the worst. But it didn't happen.

It is when we believe we are invulnerable that we are the most vulnerable of all. What all this teaches us about markets is that, when a majority seems convinced that almost nothing can go wrong, the seeds of destruction are already eating away at the underbelly of the market. Later, when things appear to not be *able* to get any worse, the recovery is beginning, because people are already taking counter-action.

FOSTERING ROBOT THINKING

Mass communication is at best a mixed blessing. We all read the same press reports, watch the same TV news programs, read the same magazines. We watch television news programs with the mistaken idea that we are gaining a pretty good total view of what is happening, instead of merely a few sound bites of news that if reported in its many faceted totality would take several hours. This atmosphere of sameness tends to shape our views of the world and give us nearly identical reactions—if that is largely what we base our opinions on. It's "natural."

It seems so convenient when we find our neighbor agrees with our views; we don't bother with probing the origin and soundness of our own ideas or our news sources.

As governments grow bigger, and media outlets merge into conglomerates, the messages that bombard us are ever more like those coming from a super-state propaganda machine. Even nonpolitical and nonpartisan thought becomes stereotyped and we feel we should believe it. After all, doesn't it come from people who are said to be experts in these matters?

ACQUIRE A SKEPTICAL MIND

I said at the start of this chapter that being contrary to *every* opinion is extreme. However, it keeps you in training, mentally, to say, "Oh, yeah?" to all the pronouncements of leaders and journalists reporting on business and government. Remember the self-interest behind them. More often than not, they contain such slanted information that you are generally ahead of the game if you reject it, not as being all false necessarily, but as being a distorted or overly simplistic image of the true picture. A half-truth can amount to a lie.

Any form of contrary opinion is healthy for the mind. Of course, before you invest or sell on the basis of contrary opinion views, you must be sure you are dealing with the truly majority view, and not just "contrariness" on your part.

STEP UP YOUR THINKING POWER

Thinking is hard work; the very hardest, some say But it's necessary work if you want to survive and prosper in today's world. And *clear* thinking automatically calls for *original* premises, which can never come from just accepting what others are telling you to think.

When you put these two facts together, they speak for themselves:

1. Most people remain no better than middle class in every country, all their lives.
2. Most people think for themselves, instead of simply absorbing the prevailing opinions, less than 1% of the time.

And contrary thinking gives freedom to thought and loosens it from the chains of simple acceptance. So, in this sense, contrary thinking is an essential part of freedom.

Part VII
PREDICTIONS AND CONCLUSIONS

"The study of history is a powerful antidote to contemporary arrogance. It is humbling to discover how many of our glib assumptions, which seem to us novel and plausible, have been tested before, not once but many times and in innumerable guises; and discovered to be at great human cost, wholly false."

Paul Johnson (historian)

19
The Past is Prologue

"Remember that the future is neither ours nor wholly not ours, so that we may neither count on it as sure to come nor abandon hope of it certain not to be."

Epicurus, 3rd century BC

Let me state at the outset that this chapter is not about predictions of the sort I make in my monthly newsletter or my *Weekly Market Update*. In these publications, I am able to give, buy, and sell points and discuss more exactly where markets are likely to be headed. I only have to be right for between 1–8 weeks. A book has a very different time horizon. The goal of this chapter, therefore, is not to pontificate where markets and the economy will be a few years from now, but to offer some context within which you can construct your own evolving model or perspective, as events and stock market action cause a change in view. And, if I have done my job successfully, you now have the tools to adjust this model to fit an ever-evolving picture.

Let me reiterate that what moves markets is how profitable underlying companies are. Economics moves markets over the longer term. When you buy a stock, you are not just buying a piece of paper and betting against somebody else on the direction of that stock. You are buying part of a business, which in turn is tied to the economy. In the last 10 years, this link between the real economy and stock prices seems to have been forgotten.

TAKING A VIEW

At the beginning of 2002, a number of advisors are suggesting that it won't be long before the uptrend that began in 1990 resumes. I disagree, not about the possibility of a new uptrend beginning in 2002–3, but in the type of up-move that might be. In Chapter 3, we talk about "Taking a View." If one "takes a view" of the last 20 years, the bear markets of 1982, 1987, and 1990 were mini-bear markets within a major bull market. But implicit in the idea that this recession could be over by mid-2002 is the belief that the excesses of the past 10 years have:

(a)   Not appreciably affected the internal structure of either the stock market or the economy.

(b)   That all the reasons that sustained the bull market that began in 1982 are still valid. That the declines over the past 2 years have wiped out all the excesses of a bubble market, and bad dot-com business plans, in exactly the same way the deliberate squeezing of inflation out of the economy did in 1981–82.

(c)   That the war on terrorism will be (in a fighting sense) an instant war, like the Gulf War, with a rapid end and all fighting/war strategies will work fairly well. I believe that all three premises are wrong, and I will deal with (a) and (b) in this chapter and (c) in Chapter 20.

PAST MAJOR BULL MARKETS

Before we further consider what the next few years might be like, we need to look at past major bull markets to examine their similarities after past boom periods. There are two such periods that share some resemblance to the 20-year period to 2000. They are: 1921 to 1929, and 1942–1966.

1921–1929 COMPARED TO 1980–2000

The 1914–18 war, known as the Great War, was the war to end all wars. It had relegated war to the status of an historical relic. The effects of winning World War I had a similar effect on the American psyche that the release of the Iranian hostages and the confidence in the future of America that Ronald Reagan was able to create. The year 1921 had a lot in common with 1981 in that post-war inflation was squeezed out of the economy, in a short sharp recession, enabling the boom of the 1920s to occur in a low inflationary environment. Like the 1980s and 1990s, nothing seemed impossible. The new technology of electricity, the automobile, and radio was transforming people's lives in ways they could only imagine. They were so convinced that the panics of the past were as much historical relics, as war was, that they labeled their times, a "New Era." The belief that nothing could go wrong gave rise to questionable business ethics and practices where the basic laws of economics were ignored in favor of simply making money by whatever means. They had their New Era bucket shops who sold stock that did not exist. We had our New Economy cyber pirates who talked up the price of stocks in order to make money off unsuspecting investors. As the 1920s wore on, and it seemed so easy to make money, few people cared that some of the new businesses based on electricity, the assembly line, and the new communication medium of radio had unsound business plans. In the 1990s, the euphoria over the Internet caused otherwise sensible people to buy stocks in new dot-com businesses that set up web sites, but were not even sure what they were going to sell on them. Both eras were fueled by a belief in the power of technology to create permanent prosperity and Utopian living, regardless of the fundamentals of individual businesses or the inflated level of stock prices.

1920s COMPARED TO 1990s

By now, you may be thinking that because the 1920s were so similar in mood to the 1980s and 1990s that the next decade has to look like the 1930s. Would that prediction was that simple! The only thing we can be sure of is that the next decade will not be an identical twin, but we can use some parts of past models to construct our model for the future. So, to continue the comparison.

Though the 1980s did not begin with a conventional military victory, that Reagan obtained the release of the Iranian hostages and raised optimism that the Cold War would soon be over created a mood of "building a better world," which made it acceptable to risk causing a recession, in order to squeeze the inflation out of the economy, making 1981 comparable to 1921.

Then, in 1989, the Berlin Wall came down, for which there is no exact past comparison. The Cold War was over and America had won. For the first time in its over 200 year history, America was the sole world superpower, similar to Britain until World War II, or similar to ancient Rome 2000 years ago. The feeling of superiority and invulnerability was palpable. Francis Fukuyama's *The End of History and the Last Man* stated, in essence, that the Cold War had been a war of ideas. American ideas had won and communist ideas had lost. It was therefore only a matter of time, he said, before the entire world adopted the American system of government and her principles of freedom. It became an instant best seller.

Although Europeans felt tremendous excitement at the fall of the Berlin Wall, for much of the Cold War they had been bystanders, hoping desperately that neither America nor the USSR would do anything to start a nuclear war, which would be largely fought on their territory. Hence, though Europeans felt relief and empathy towards their newly-freed Eastern neighbors, there was none of the feeling of "justification by heaven" for their system of government and way of life that pervaded America after 1989. A feeling that was multiplied by the precision bombing and declared victory of the war against Iraq in 1991. The euphoric mood in the US during the early 1990s began to match that of the 1920s.

During the 1980s, as the possibility of a nuclear war became less of a threat, the Internet, which had originally been designed so that military commanders in the field could communicate with headquarters, was expanded to allow limited civilian use, mainly by those involved in defense research or indirectly with military operations.

After 1989, the Internet was released for civilian use. But it was not until 1993 that the World Wide Web, as we now know it, began to become part of our general consciousness. And, by 1994, the potential of the commercial uses for the Internet began to be realized.

If you look at the 70-year chart of the Dow (Figure 19.1), you will see that 1994 was the year that the trend line of the Average became much steeper. Had the Internet been just a new technology, it is probable that it would not have caused this acute increase in the incline of the trend line. But, by 1994, the cumulative effect of first the great Communicator Reagan giving Americans back their pride, lost during Vietnam, followed by the victory of the Cold War, and Desert Storm, gave the Internet an almost religious significance to a growing audience.

Americans had won the Cold War. It was only a matter of time before her ideals of egalitarianism and freedom became globally accepted as self-evident truths, and the Internet would be the Holy Place where the spirit of liberty and equality could flourish and be proselytized.

There was nothing ethically or morally wrong with this attitude. It was just that it was a too *simplistic* and *naive* reading of the events of the 1980s and early 1900s, which in turn caused the unrealistic expectations of what the Internet as technology, as opposed to Internet as religion, could accomplish in the economic sphere.

The rest, as they say, is history. The bubble burst in early 2000, and, for over a year before the World Trade Center attack, markets had been trending downward. Therefore, if any comparison can be made between 1929–42 and 2000–10, it is to point out that the period 1929–32 will not replicate this time around, even if a few similarities occur. From 1929 until the low in 1932, government did everything wrong. Had they have just stayed out of the way, it is likely, after the initial panic that took the Dow from 381 to 200, that after a short rally the market would have trended slowly sideways to down to about 100 over a period of maybe 5 years. This in turn would have been a lot less destructive to the economic infrastructure of the country. But Herbert Hoover was a stubborn ideologue, who thought he had the answers to the nation's problems and by sheer force of will persuaded the Federal Reserve, Congress, and industrial leaders to take action, which made an already shaky situation much worse.

But, before I compare the rest of the 1930s to the period to 2010, I wish to make one other comparison with the past.

1950s AND 1960s COMPARED TO 1990s

Like the end of the Cold War, at the end of World War II, a great deal of technology, developed to fight the war, was released for civilian use. But World War II was very different to the Cold War in that Americans were forced to make sacrifices. Rationing was instituted. The men were shipped out, while the women manned the factories. And though, after Pearl Harbor, the war was not fought on American soil, the entire country was aware that war has a price, and in this instance a price that had to be paid.

When war was over, the GIs returned to build a better world at home. But, there was not that feeling of entitlement or invulnerability that occurred after the end of the Cold War, a war in which Americans had not been asked to sacrifice. For this reason, while the mood was optimistic during the 1950s, it was not irrationally so. And the Korean War, which took up much of the 1950s, constantly reminded Americans that, though they had beaten Hitler, another potential threat was rising.

By the late 1950s, the technology from World War II had been absorbed into the economy, and there seemed nothing new on the horizon to keep the economy moving upwards. Apparently, the USSR sensed this slowing in the US, and they installed missiles, pointing at the US, in Cuba. But Kennedy faced down the Soviets, first in Cuba and then in Berlin, when the Wall was erected, which restored American confidence sufficiently to carry the stock market up to its 1966 high. In addition to the confidence inspired by Kennedy's actions, some major new technology was coming on stream that helped fuel the rise. That of electronics and transistors. Towards the end of the 1960s, this new technology created an irrational exuberance, akin to that which the Internet caused. And a similar result occurred in 1969, 1970, when many new high-tech companies lost much of their value, while some went out of business.

But, the 1960s were a lot more complicated than the 1990s. In 1966, the Vietnam War began, and the new technology, which enabled war for the first time to be beamed into civilian living rooms, made it a highly unpopular war. The only way government could pacify an angry electorate and continue to fight a war, which Linden Johnson, as big an ideologue as Warren Harding had been, believed needed to be fought, was to prove to the public that this war would not ask them to sacrifice. It was his "guns and butter" policy, more than the Arab oil embargo in 1973, that caused the double-digit inflation of the 1970s. If low inflation had been maintained throughout the 1960s, the economy would have been able to more or less ride out the oil crisis, with

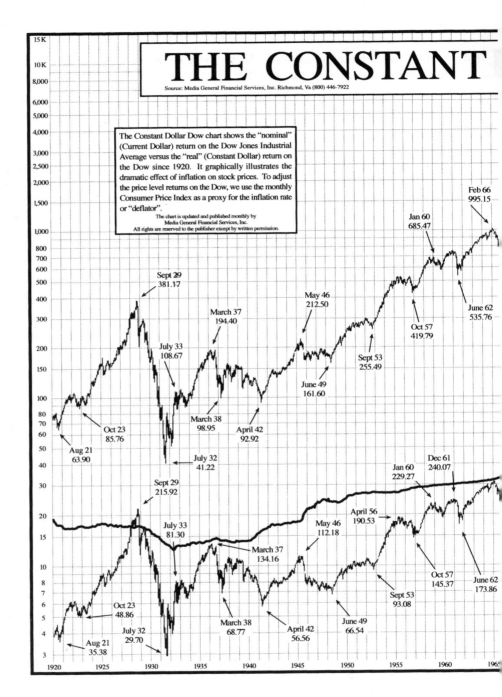

The Constant Dollar Dow chart shows the "nominal" (Current Dollar) return on the Dow Jones Industrial Average versus the "real" (Constant Dollar) return on the Dow since 1920. It graphically illustrates the dramatic effect of inflation on stock prices. To adjust the price level returns on the Dow, we use the monthly Consumer Price Index as a proxy for the inflation rate or "deflator".

The chart is updated and published monthly by
Media General Financial Services, Inc.
All rights are reserved to the publisher except by written permission.

THE CONSTANT

Source: Media General Financial Services, Inc. Richmond, Va (800) 446-7922

Figure 19.1. The Constant Dollar Dow.

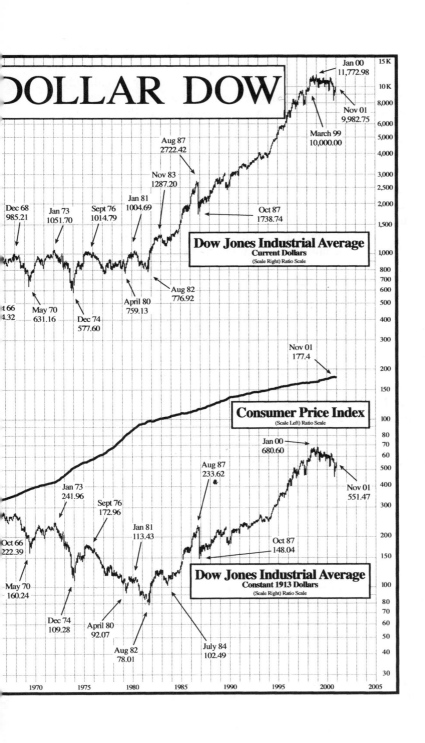

DOLLAR DOW

Jan 00
11,772.98

Nov 01
9,982.75

March 99
10,000.00

Aug 87
2722.42

Nov 83
1287.20

Jan 81
1004.69

Oct 87
1738.74

Dec 68
985.21

Jan 73
1051.70

Sept 76
1014.79

Dow Jones Industrial Average
Current Dollars
(Scale Right) Ratio Scale

Aug 82
776.92

t 66
4.32

May 70
631.16

Dec 74
577.60

April 80
759.13

Nov 01
177.4

Consumer Price Index
(Scale Left) Ratio Scale

Jan 00
680.60

Nov 01
551.47

Jan 73
241.96

Sept 76
172.96

Aug 87
233.62

Jan 81
113.43

Oct 87
148.04

Oct 66
222.39

May 70
160.24

Dow Jones Industrial Average
Constant 1913 Dollars
(Scale Right) Ratio Scale

Dec 74
109.28

April 80
92.07

July 84
102.49

Aug 82
78.01

moderate inflationary damage. But, by 1973, the money supply was already so out of control that the OPEC jolt simply exacerbated an already inflationary situation. So how do the 1960s compare with where we are at the beginning of 2002?

There are some similarities, as well as some big differences. Like the latter part of the 1960s, the Federal Reserve has, for the last 2 years, been pumping huge amounts of what is euphemistically called "liquidity" into the system. The difference has been in consumer sentiment.

Since the collapse of the overvalued market in early 2000, the Fed cut interest rates more aggressively than was done in the late 1960s. But, the impact on the stock market and the economy was almost nil during the year of non-stop cuts. Yet, in the late 1960s, pump priming drove the Dow back up to its 1966 high, both in 1968 and again in 1973. Why the difference? In the 1960s and 1970s, consumers were willing to spend with abandon. Since early 2000, this has not been the case. Therefore, it is also "probably" safe to say that, between 2002 and 2010, we will not see the kind of double-digit inflation that we saw during the 1970s because, even if the Fed cuts interest rates to zero, consumers can't be forced to spend more.

Inflation does not occur just because the rates at which the consumer can borrow money are low. Inflation will occur when, as a result of low interest rates, consumers shop till they drop and increase their debt exposure. So far, that has not happened. And the September 11, 2001 attack has dampened consumer desire to spend further.

A POSSIBLE MODEL FOR THE FUTURE

By now, you should realize that although the next few years will have some similarities with the 1930s and the 1970s, it won't be an exact replica of either of them. The roaring twenties public, who had bought stocks with abandon up until 1929, never did come back into the market during the 1930s. That doesn't mean that the 1930s were a period of unmitigated economic gloom and bear markets. They weren't. There was a sizable bull market from 1932–37, when the Dow increased 268% over a 5-year period. But, it exhibited none of the froth or exuberance of the late 1920s.

Likewise, in the 16 years from 1966 to 1982; although the Dow never did manage to better its 1966 high, there were four mama-size bull markets, with tops in 1968, 1973, 1979, and 1981. But none of these bull markets compared with that which ended in 1966. The swinging sixties investor was either wiped out by the fall in their high-tech stocks by 1969, or they decided to use their money in other areas. They weren't buying stocks during the 1970s.

I therefore have no quarrel with my fellow advisors who predict a new bull market in the fairly near future. My only quarrel is with those who suggest that any new bull market will merely be a resumption of the late great bull market of the last 10 years. The irrationally exuberant 1990s are over. The New Economy investors have been wiped out, scared out of the market, or are still grimly holding on in hopes the market will come back. The latter will only sell out when/if they need the money for other things. And, in fact, there never was a "New Economy." That was a catchy phrase used to run stock prices up beyond their real values.

There is sufficient damage to the infrastructure of the economy, both in the US and abroad, that it cannot be resolved in a "V bottom" leading to a resumption of the uptrend, as some are predicting.

The US *economy* was already in a bear market and a shallow recession before September 11, 2001. And previously, for at least two prior years, the more high-flying high-tech companies had been going out of business. We may indeed be in the early stages of the most globally synchronized depression since the 1930s, as *The Economist* stated in its August 25, 2001 edition, but it will not look like either the 1930s or the 1970s. Yet, it will have similarities to both eras.

TO SUM UP

Prediction is an inexact science at best. And more difficult than predicting *where* the market will go is trying to guess *when* it will do it. So, it's brazen to forecast in a book. But, in my view, problems in world stock markets and global economies, barring a miracle, will not be resolved before well into 2003. And don't rule out 2005 as a long shot. There will be hefty secondary rallies in market averages, and a new mini-bull market or two. But, it will not be a resumption of the old bubble uptrend. The next 2 years plus will be a market of stocks, not a stock market. There will be a large number of individual stocks that will enjoy healthy growth, but the idea that one can buy most anything and forget about it, and it will go up, à la the last 10 years, is well and truly past. "Buy and hold" is history. My best guess for the earliest beginning of the next great bull market, of the sort we saw in the 1920s, 1950s and 1960s, or the 1980s and 1990s, is around 2005.

WILL THIS BE A DEFLATIONARY OR INFLATIONARY PERIOD?

Because of government interference in markets, this is difficult to judge at this stage. But, my best prediction is that it will be less deflationary than the 1930s, but not as inflationary as the 1970s. That assumes, of course, that OPEC and other oil producers won't suddenly decide to force up the price of oil. Though, as of this writing, it seems likely that any price increase they may manage to manipulate will be minor and have little effect on the overall inflation rate in the short term. In a worst case scenario, high single-digit inflation is not out of the question, but more would require an unforeseen event that, as of this writing, is not on the horizon. But, other things can cause inflation to rise. If consumer confidence suddenly returned, that could push price inflation up fairly quickly.

WAR ON TERRORISM IS THE KEY

How the war against terrorism plays out will be a major key, not only because of the cost of military hardware to fight a war, but because this kind of war affects the public's willingness to take risk. And, until or unless there is a clear-cut victory against terrorism of the sort we saw in 1989 when the Berlin Wall came down, it is unlikely that the former irrational exuberance for stocks will return for ages.

To oversimplify, I believe we are entering a period of economic and stock price erosion, akin to but not the same as that which existed in the 1930s and the 1970s: a period of multi-year duration. But within what can be called a major bear market, there will be substantial mini-bull markets. In order to survive and prosper during the next few years, you need to remain flexible, nimble and ever watchful, and cynical. Take nothing for granted and never forget that any model of future market action is an evolving one. What is 100% true on Tuesday may need to be modified by Friday. Constantly update your thinking and reexamine your premises for why you took a position—long or short—in a particular security.

And always remember the old Wall Street adage:

"When in doubt, get out."

20
Epilogue

"It is a profound mistake to think the horizon is the boundary of the world."

Antoine Marin Lemierre

In my newsletter, I have always taken a totally holistic approach to investing, because what is the point of making money if the country in which you live has a weak rule of law, or feeble human rights and freedoms?

Money has no value of itself. Its value is measured only in what it can do/buy. When it buys you a lifestyle in a society where the rule of law assures freedom and basic human rights for all citizens, it has great value. But if you are a billionaire, and/or a member of the elite in an autocratic regime, though money can buy you things, it cannot buy you the intangibles that even a middle-class lifestyle can in a free society.

For years my approach to investment was regarded as a little "unusual." But slowly, my holistic approach has gained acceptance, as ever more economists, even a few Nobel Laureates, no longer see their profession as a purely inductive "dismal" science, but are incorporating sociology, psychology, philosophy and, in the case of economist Robert William Fogel, 1993 Nobel Prize winner, in his book *The Fourth Great Awakening*, even religion into their economic projections!

SOCIETY IS A "RELIGIOUS PHENOMENON"

Alan Ebenstein, in his book *Friedrich Hayek*, writes:

> "The order of society is an abstract order. It is an internal vision held by members of a society as to how a society should physically look,

what patterns of relationships should exist in a society and what the material outcomes of these patterns will be. Capitalism, Hayek thought, is the physical manifestation of the historical western moral code."

In the ancient world, religion was not a set of dogmas that all must believe. It was a set of images (metaphors) that gave substance to the set of abstract values by which society operated. A kind of proto-Constitution. The word *religion* comes from a Latin word which means "to bind together." In its original meaning, religion was what today we call "civic religion," and public religious worship was a similar activity to modern nations' pledge of alliance to their flags. It was an act of solidarity with group political values, not a statement of theological belief.

In this sense, America's Founding Documents, the Communist Manifesto, *Mein Kampf*, and Mao's *Little Red Book* are as much "Scripture" as the Christian Bible, the Jewish Torah and Talmud, the Koran, and the Analects of Confucius.

But the difference between traditional religions and Religious Fundamentalism, Nazism, Fascism, and Communism is that none of the founders of the world's traditional religions were fanatics. The Talmud reads more like the *arguments* that must have gone on between America's Founders during the Constitutional Convention than a single, static absolute truth for all time. The New Testament offers four *different* Gospel perspectives on what Jesus taught, which shows that early Christians were not so much concerned with dogma as with a *general set of values*. And Mohammed was much more tolerant of other beliefs than many modern Islamic clerics.

The war that began in 1914 has been ongoing for the last 88 years. World Wars I and II, the Cold War, the Korean War, Vietnam, and the many acts of terrorism over the last 30 years are all individual battles in the one great ideological war by self-appointed leaders who believe they know how to create Utopia, who devise new civic religions by which to govern an ever-changing world. But the problem with any religion once it becomes "absolute dogma" is that it ceases to evolve. Yet, life is an evolving process.

The brilliance of America's Founders was that they were realists, not Utopians, so they put a political structure in place to offer maximum freedom, while curtailing the tendency towards anarchy. Though they may have disliked "organized" religion as much as Marx did, they supported *individual* beliefs and merely prevented any particular religious dogma from forcing people to live according to its world view. The US Founders returned religion to its ancient Roman meaning, of civic virtue rather than a control of national ideology.

UTOPIA OR JUST MUDDLING THROUGH

The term Utopia was first used by Sir Thomas More in 1516, to describe his idea of a perfect society. The word Utopia comes from two Greek words, *ou* meaning "no", and *topos* meaning "place." Hence, More's Utopia was about "no place" and was probably an ironic, even sarcastic commentary on the massive bloodshed of the Reformation, where Europeans killed one another with abandon over unprovable theological differences. But, this was the first time in history that the idea of a perfect society in this world was deemed either possible or desirable. Prior to the 16th century, life was considered a vale of tears, which if accepted and endured would guarantee a better life after death.

But, as a result of new shipping technology, new lands were discovered, and the standard of living for all Europeans increased sufficiently, that perfecting life on this planet was deemed possible and became the aim of some intellectuals and theologians. Modern Marxists and religious Fundamentalists are heirs to this transition.

The folly of this thinking is that life is an evolving, not a static enterprise, where each person has what Nobel Laureate economist Frederick Hayek calls "unique information" to contribute. This creates dynamic spiritual and economic progress. But if nations are controlled from the *center*, that progress is severely impeded, and it denies the individual the right to find his or her own salvation, to become what economist Russell Roberts calls "essentially human." Fundamentalism within traditional religions, and the modern ideologies of Communism, Fascism, Nazism, and other "isms," are all cults. They delude their followers into believing there are easy and instant answers to the problems of the human condition. But, those who espouse such answers are setting themselves up as demigods—an arrogance that all traditional scriptures condemn.

The human race learns slowly and tends to take one step backwards for every two steps forward. But, our progress over millennia *has* been upwards—though that uptrend has a more gentle gradient than we believed it to have in the somewhat self-deluding 1990s.

But, now, we are in a consolidation period—economically, socially, and politically. A time when our belief systems and social organizations are evolving to better fit a 21st century world view of Ultimate Reality.

Modern so-called secular societies are, in my view, more "religious" in the traditional sense than the cultist self-styled saviors of society, whether they be members of al Qaeda, Iranian clerics, communist revolutionaries, or those Christian Fundamentalists who bombed abortion clinics, or the Federal building in Oklahoma in 1995.

All new religions are accused of being atheist or secular when they first appear, because they see Ultimate Reality in more abstract terms. Early Christians were accused of being atheists because they refused to worship the many very human-like gods of the ancient world, and instead worshipped an abstract God and a dead Jewish teacher.

Secular societies who encourage *all* religions, but favor none, are more, not less religious than theocracies like Iran, Israel, or the recently deposed Taliban government.

Whatever our personal beliefs, we should never lose sight of the fact that government is not, and can never be, an all-knowing God-like caretaker. Utopia can never be achieved. The most we can do, as economist David Landes says in *The Wealth and Poverty of Nations*, is:

> "The one lesson that emerges is the need to keep trying. No miracles. No perfection. No apocalypse. We must cultivate a skeptical faith, avoid dogma, listen and watch well, try to clarify and define ends, the better to choose means."

America's Founders would have agreed. They built in checks and balances to prevent government from setting itself up as god-like, or claiming to rule by divine right. The US lack of political/religious dogma, while specifically defining society's basic values, has given America unparalleled dynamism over the last 200 years—because it gave every American room to become "fully human."

We must never forget that the society we have in the West is not and never can be Utopia, nor the final answer to individual freedom. Though it achieves the greatest prosperity combined with the greatest (relative) freedom of any generally known and accepted systems of government, *it is only the best we have come up with so far*!

Our system of government is, as Churchill put it in 1947, "The worst form of government except all those other forms that have been tried from time to time."

Only if we keep this in mind, and constantly adjust our societies, using the special knowledge that each of us have, will we continue (on balance), to advance in prosperity and relative freedom. And only then will there be free securities markets for us to invest in, and a world where we will want to spend our profits.

And if I have done my job well in this book, you dear reader, will be ready to buy at the start of a new, hopefully long-term period of stability and economic growth, which will not only make you richer, but which will enable you to buy a truly fulfilling lifestyle in a world where increasingly the rule of law and basic human rights will be part of national constitutions. Meantime, enjoy bear market opportunities when they occur. They too can provide prosperity.

Glossary of Terms and Tactics for Market Mastery

Advance/Decline (A/D) Line: A line created from the difference between the number of stocks that went up and the number that went down for each trading day (on a weekly basis). Stocks unchanged are not counted. Shows what the great mass of stocks are doing, in contrast to the limited number of stocks contained in any stock index. It's especially noteworthy when it diverges from the stock averages, particularly the S&P or DJIA. If the Dow is making new highs while the A/D line is falling, it shows that only a few stocks are "leading the market," making new Dow highs suspect and increasing the odds of a reversal.

American Depository Receipt (ADR): Instruments issued by US banks as counterparts for non-US securities. In practice, they are the same as shares of a corporation, except ADRs are traded on a US exchange, not the exchange in which the corporation is domiciled. Are also used for international arbitrage when price of ADR diverges from price of stock in country where domiciled.

At-the-Money: An option that has a strike price the same as, or very close to, the market value of the underlying security.

Automatic Reinvestment: Automatic reinvestment of shareholder dividends in a corporation's stock. The corporation usually does this without brokerage fees and may even offer a small discount from the current price.

Average Down: To buy more at a lower price than the original purchase. For example, if you bought shares at 100 and later buy more at 90, you "averaged down." Not recommended unless an experienced investor. But a tactic that can turn a loss into a gain, especially if adept at discerning chart support and resistance levels.

Average Up: (1) To sell more at a higher price than the original purchase. For example, you sold short at 70. If you sell more short at 80 you "averaged up." Not recommended unless an experienced investor. (2) Infrequently used to describe additional buying at higher prices.

Basis Point: (1) 0.01% of yield in a fixed-income security. For example, if the T-Bond yield drops from 7.05% to 6.40%, it's declined 65 basis points. (2) Used in referring to changes in price in other than fixed-income securities. For example, if Yen futures drop from 98.10 to 95.50, the drop will normally be described as 260 "ticks" rather than basis points.

Bearish: Having the opinion a market is going to go down.

Bearish Divergence: Most commonly, a new high in price without a corresponding new high in a related price, average, index, or other technical indicator. For example, if a stock makes a new high, but a technical indicator doesn't, it points to a loss of upward momentum and possible correction or change in trend.

Beta: A measure of a stock's volatility in comparison to the S&P 500 index. The S&P 500 index is given a value of 1. If a stock is more volatile than the S&P, it will have a beta greater than 1. If less volatile, the beta will be less than 1. For example, if the S&P 500 index moves 5%, a stock that usually moves at 7.5% will have a beta of 1.50, indicating that it's 1.5 times as volatile as the S&P. Betas are useful in constructing portfolios of greater or lesser volatility than the S&P 500 index.

Bid/Ask Spread: The difference in price at which you can buy and sell. For example, if a stock has a bid/ask spread of "159 at $159\frac{1}{4}$," you'd pay $159\frac{1}{4}$ if buying and receive 159 if selling. The Bid/Ask spread is not unique to financial markets. If you were to purchase a numismatic coin from a coin dealer, you'd pay the Ask price. If you wanted to sell the same coin to the dealer, you'd receive the Bid price. The Bid/Ask spread is the price of doing business in any market in which you are not in the business yourself. Also called Bid/Offer spread.

Blue Chip: A term originally designating a chip off a blue stone—a diamond. The term was also adopted for high-value poker chips. It's used to describe shares of first class corporations—those which are large and have a good record of earnings and paying dividends. They're usually old and well established. However, their prices go down as well as up, so don't expect to escape a major bear market by only buying blue-chip stocks.

Bond: A long-term debt instrument issued by a government or corporation. The term in years of various bonds varies, but is usually 5–10 years. Can be longer. Debt instruments with a shorter term than 5 years, but over 1 year, are usually referred to as Notes.

Bullish: Having the opinion a market (in anything) is going to go up.

Bullish Consensus: Generically, a survey and compilation of the percentage of advisors or investment areas that are bullish or bearish. A number of companies do these surveys on a daily and weekly basis. *Investor's Intelligence* is a widely followed stock-market consensus. Market Vane's *Bullish Consensus* is widely followed in future markets.

Bullish Divergence: Most commonly, a new low in price without a corresponding new low in a related price, average, index, or other technical indicator. For example, if a stock makes a new high, but a technical indicator such as Stochastics doesn't, it points to a loss of downward momentum and possible correction or change in trend.

Buy backs: Some companies buy-back their stock in the open market. This reduces the number of shares outstanding, which in theory increases the net earnings per share. The ethics is debatable and the SEC (Securities and Exchange Commission) frowned on it in 2000 and early 2001, though they OKed it to help the US stock market after September 11. Buy backs are illegal in many countries, and in my opinion should be in all. It's an artificial way of growing earnings, aimed at giving the appearance of higher earnings even though the company did not increase their sales. A major drawback is that companies use up their cash reserves this way and can find themselves cash short when business declines or is in a recession.

Call (Option): (1) A type of option. A call option gives the buyer the right but not the obligation to buy a stated number of shares of a security at a stated price on or before a specified date. (Also used for bonds and futures contracts.) For example, a December 85 stock call option gives the owner the right to buy 100 shares of that stock on or before the December expiration date of the option (usually the third Friday of the month) at 85 regardless of the actual price of the stock at the time. More frequently, if the option is "in the money" (i.e., the stock is above the 85 strike price), the owner will simply sell the option and collect the profit. If the stock is below 85 and/or the option expires, the call buyer loses all of the money (premium) paid for the option. The advantage of buying options is leverage. For several hundred dollars, you have the right for a limited time to participate in the advance of a stock, which if you bought the stock directly would require a much larger investment. The big disadvantage is that you not only have to be right about the direction of price movement, your timing must also be correct. (2) The action by which a company decides to redeem a security before its maturity date.

Cancel/Replace: Canceling an order and replacing it with a different order for the same security or contract.

Cash Charts: Price charts reflecting the cash or "spot" price of a commodity in comparison to a forward price in the futures market.

Chicago Board of Trade: US futures exchange on which financial instruments (T-Bonds, T-Notes, Municipal bonds) and the Grain Complex (corn, oats, soybeans, etc.) are traded. Called CBT.

Chicago Mercantile Exchange (CME): US futures exchange on which the S&P index, cattle, and pork bellies are traded. A division of the CME, the International Money Market (IMM), trades currency futures and the Eurodollar.

Closed-End (Mutual) Fund: An investment company that manages a mutual fund with a *limited* and fixed number of shares. Listed on an exchange, it is very similar to a stock, in that you can place buy and sell orders, stop-loss orders, limit orders, etc., which are not possible in an open-end fund.

Commodity Exchange Inc. (COMEX): US futures exchange on which copper, gold, and silver are traded.

Common Stock: A security representing an ownership interest in a corporation. Common stock holders have claims on assets of the company only after claims of bondholders, other creditors and preferred-stock holders. Common stockholders control management and company policy via voting rights.

Confirm: To validate or increase the validity of a particular market movement, usually a new or significant high or low. For example, if the Dow makes a new high but the Dow Jones Transports do not, the new high is not "confirmed." Can also use it with other market indices (e.g., A/D line). More generally, confirmation has to do with comparing a number of technical indicators or studies to see if most are in agreement as to future price movement.

Contingency order: An order that depends/is contingent upon some other parameter occurring first, usually the execution of another order.

Contrary Opinion: A market theory based on the concept that the "crowd" is usually wrong. A contrary opinion is a minority opinion (and a small minority at that) that is the opposite of what most people think will occur.

Convertible Bond: A bond that can be converted into common shares at a price or rate and/or date specified upon issuance of the bond.

Correction: Any temporary reversal or retracement in price movement in the opposite direction of the price movement/trend that just occurred. Normally used when referring to a price movement not in the direction of the medium term or primary trends.

Cover: The action of buying after initially selling (shorting).

Day Order: All orders are considered "day" orders unless specifically stated otherwise. Day orders are good for that trading session only and expire at the end of the trading session.

Divergence: Failure of the price movement of one security, average, index, or technical indicator to confirm the price movement of another security, average, index, or technical indicator.

Diversification: The reduction of risk by investing in non-related securities and different types of investment, such as stocks (or stock groups), bonds, CDs, money market accounts, currencies, precious metals, etc. Risk spreading ensures that if an area goes sour, one may still be doing well in another.

Dividend: Payments made by corporations to their shareholders in cash or stock, out of corporate earnings.

Dow Jones Industrial Average (DJIA): A market average of 30 widely-held NYSE-listed stocks. It is not weighted for capitalization of the stocks. It is computed by taking the sum of the prices of the 30 stocks and dividing by an adjusted denominator. As the denominator gets smaller, the volatility of the Dow increases. The DJIA is the world's most widely followed and quoted stock market index, but increasingly the S&P is preferred as more representative.

Dow Jones Transportation Average (DJTA): Originally the Rail Average, the DJTA is composed of 20 stocks consisting of airlines, freight, railroads, etc.

Earnings Per Share (EPS): A corporation's net income after taxes and payments to preferred shareholders divided by the number of outstanding shares of stock.

Emerging Markets: Markets in countries that are not well established economically/financially, but are making progress in that direction.

Eurodollar: US dollars on deposit at European banks and used for overseas business transactions.

Ex-Dividend Date: When a stock trades "ex-dividend," it means on that day a dividend was paid on the share and this amount is deducted from the share price.

Fundamental Analysis: One of the two broad categories of market analysis (the other is technical) used to obtain indications of future price movements. It is based on a company's balance sheet, profit and loss statement, earnings, industry trends, economic and managerial data, supply and demand of product, etc.

Futures: A contract that contains an agreement to buy a specific amount of a commodity or financial instrument at a particular price on a stipulated date. It obligates the buyer to purchase and the seller to sell, unless the contract is offset before the settlement date.

Gap: A span in price between the close of the previous trading session, and the open of the subsequent trading session, either up or down.

GTC: Good till canceled order. Means what it says. *See also* Open Order.

Gilts: Securities of corporations that have shown over time their ability to pay continuous dividends or interest. Most commonly used to describe bonds.

In-the-Money: Phrase used to describe any option in which there is intrinsic value. That is, the amount the market price of the underlying security is above the option's strike price in call options. For put options: The amount the market price of the underlying security is below the option's strike price.

Leverage: In the financial sense, making a given amount of money do more work than is normal (e.g., buying stock on margin, or buying options rather than the underlying stock).

Long Bond: A bond maturing in more than 10 years.

Margin: (1) A loan from a broker to buy stock, hence buying stock "on margin." Loan is usually up to 50% of the price of the stock purchased. (2) Good-faith deposit on a futures contract.

Margin Call: A broker's request for you to put up more money (margin) because your stock/bond/futures have dropped below your margin. If you don't come up with more money, or sell some of your position, the broker will sell all or part to meet the call. It is also a wake-up call that something is very wrong! It is usually a sign the account is undercapitalized, and/or you are not using stop losses to limit losses, and/or you are over-leveraging your investments, often a problem with having too many futures contracts.

Market Order: An order filled as soon as possible at the best obtainable price at that time.

MIT (Market If Touched) Order: Used mainly in futures markets. An MIT order becomes a market order when the specified price is reached.

MOC (Market On Close) Order: An order to be filled at the end of the session. Usually in the last 30 seconds of trading in equities or last 2 minutes in futures.

MOO (Market On Open) Order: Works the same as an MOC order except it is executed when the market opens.

Moving Average: Average price of a security, index, etc. over a period of time. For example, a 39-week moving average is the sum of the last 39 weeks' closing prices divided by 39. Each week, the oldest price is dropped and the current price added before the average is retotaled.

Not-Held: (1) A stipulation by a broker that he or she is not held responsible if an order is not executed, or not executed at the desired price. The order is accepted solely on a "best efforts" basis with no guarantees whatsoever. (2) A qualifier that allows floor brokers to use their discretion with respect to the time and price of an order's execution.

Open Order: An order that doesn't expire at the end of a trading session. An open order will remain active until the order is executed, canceled, or changed. Some brokerages limit the time they'll keep an open order (e.g., 30 days). So, when you place an open order, check how long it will be valid for. *See also* GTC.

Open-End (Mutual) Fund: A management investment company in which new shares are issued according to supply and demand of investors. Not listed on stock exchanges. Biggest drawback is inability to place stop-loss orders. Also, some require notice before withdrawing shares. Selling "at the market" mid-session is not usually possible.

Open Interest: Total number of options or futures contracts that have not been liquidated. An open interest figure represents both the buyer and seller of a particular option or futures contract.

Overbought: Term used to describe a security that has advanced appreciably and for which the probability of a corrective decline is high. Many technical oscillators, such as Stochastics, are used to try to determine at what point an overbought condition exists.

Oversold: Describes a security that has declined appreciably and in which the probability of a corrective rally is high.

Penny Stock: A relatively low-priced, highly-speculative security. Loosely defined as any stock under $5, but traditionally under $1.

Preferred Stock: Part of the stock of a corporation that has priority over common stock in the distribution of dividends. In the event of a bankruptcy, preferred stock holders are ahead of common stock holders with regard to the distribution of assets.

Premium: The price of an option consisting of the sum of its time value and intrinsic value.

Price–Earnings Ratio: The quotient obtained by dividing a stock's current market price by the current yearly earnings per common share. Also called "multiple."

Pyramiding: Adding to your position in a particular security, often using profits from an earlier purchase. For example, if your initial purchase was at 30, and the share rises to 40, you buy more.

Record Date: Date on which a shareholder must own shares in order to receive the next dividend.

Resistance: A price level or range of prices at which a security stopped advancing in the past or is anticipated to stop advancing should it rise to that level in the future.

Shorting Against the Box: A short sale. If, near the end of a tax year, you feel a certain stock you own might go down in price and it ought to be sold, but you do not want to pay the capital gains tax in that year, you can short it your long against the box. You sell short the same number of shares as you hold long. Thus, you lock in your profit without actually selling your stock.

Short Squeeze: A situation in which traders who have sold short feel forced (by rising prices) to buy to cover their short positions. The amount of "forced" buying drives prices even higher than they would normally go.

Stochastics: A technical indicator that functions as an overbought/oversold oscillator. It is based on the premise that when a price is rising, it will tend to close near the high of the day on daily charts. For an advance to stop, it must first slow down. Thus a change in the momentum of an advance occurs before the price reverses. Stochastics attempts to identify this change in momentum.

Stock Split: (1) Forward split: An increase in the number of shares of a corporation without any change in the shareholder's equity. Usually done to make a stock more marketable by reducing its price. (2) Reverse split: A decrease in the number of shares of a corporation without any change in the shareholder's equity. Done to raise the price of a stock, usually to above the level of a "penny stock."

Strike Price: The stated price of an option at which the owner can buy the underlying security in the case of a call option or sell in the case of a put option.

Unit Trust: Same as Open-End Mutual Fund. British term.

Yield: General term for the percentage return on an investment.

Resources

RECOMMENDED INVESTMENT NEWSLETTERS

I would be remiss if I didn't tell you about my own newsletter, which has been published continuously for 38 years:

- *International Harry Schultz Letter* (also known as *Harry Schultz Life Strategies*). Mail to: *HSL*, PO Box 622, CH-1001, Lausanne, Switzerland. Subscription phone: (506) 234 0433, fax: (506) 234 0433 (that's in Costa Rica) and email: HSLmentor@racsa.co.cr

If you wish to contact me personally please fax me at (377) 97 70 31 48 (that's in Monte Carlo) or email me at cameleon1@compuserve.com

- *The Aden Forecast*, Dept 874, PO Box 025216, Miami, FL 33102-5216, email: adenres@racsa.co.cr Offers general stock and metals analysis, plus currency commentary with charts.
- *Currency Bulletin, John Pervical*. Info: www.currencybulletin.com Sophisticated currencies (only) analysis.
- *Daily Reckoning Investment Advisory, Bill Bonner*. US phone: 800-433-1528, or (978) 514-7857 email: dailyreckoning.com Wide-ranging views and news on markets.
- *Dick Davis Digest*. US fax: 800 654-3659. Gives excerpts from various newsletters of stock recommendations.
- *Dow Theory Letters, Richard Russell*, PO Box 1758, La Jolla, California 92038, email: staff@dowtheoryletters.com Foremost theoretician for Dow Theory in its fullest measure. Conservative.
- *Elliott Wave International, Robert Prechter*, PO Box 1618, Gainesville, Georgia 30503, phone: (770) 536 0309, website: www.elliottwave.com Exceptional Elliott Wave specialist.

- *FullerMoney, David Fuller*, Suite 1.21, Plaza 535 Kings Road, London
  SW10 0SZ, UK, email: research@fullermarkets.com websites:
  www.fullermoney.com www.chartanalysts.com Highly-skillful chart
  analysis. Also produces charts.
- *Gloom, Boom & Doom Report, Marc Faber*. Fax Hong Kong: (852)
  2526-0378 Zeroes in on economics and markets in essay form.
- *Growth Stock Outlook, Charles Allmon*, PO Box 15381, Chevy Chase, MD
  20815. Stocks picks using fundamental analysis.
- *Gold & Tech Stocks, J. Taylor*, PO Box 770871, Woodside, NY 11377,
  phone: (718) 457 1426 Stock recommendations and strong gold advocacy
  essays.
- *Investment Bulletin, J. and V. Heffernan*, 1 Fern Dene, Clevelands, Ealing,
  London, W13 8AN, UK Covers British stocks in detail.
- *Long & Short, G. Payne*, 180 Cypress Club Drive, Pompano Beach, FL
  33060 Stock recommendations, long and short. Fibonacci-oriented.
- *McAlvany Intelligence Advisor, Don McAlvany*, PO Box 84804, Phoenix,
  AZ 85071, phone: 800 528 0559 Outspoken, comprehensive commentary
  on economics, politics, morality. A gold advocate.
- *The Granville Market Letter*, PO Drawer 413006, Kansas City, MO 64141
  Original-thinking stock-market technician.
- *The Reaper, R. E. McMaster*. Info: www.TheReaper.com Deep thinking
  on cogent economic/social matters plus specific futures/stock advisory.

In keeping with our holistic approach to investing, we also recommend the
following:

Political Newsletters

- *The Conservative Caucus, Howard Phillips*, 422 Maple Ave, E Vienna, VA
  22180 Strongly conservative, no compromise. A principled political
  newsletter.
- *Straight Talk, Tom Anderson*, Woodland Terrace, 300 Kildaire Woods
  Drive, Cary, NC 26511 A political newsletter with a libertarian viewpoint.
  He pulls no punches.

Health Newsletters

- *Coleman Health Letter*, PO Box 60, Barnstaple, Devon, UK. Is stridently
  anti-establishment. Is critical of the established medical and political
  hierarchy.
- *McAlvany Health Alert*, PO Box 849C4, Phoenix, AZ 85071,
  fax: 602 943 2363, phone: 602 252 4477 Most in-depth newsletter analysis
  of health problems available.

BOOKS

Basic Market Know-How and Technical Analysis

- *Technical Analysis of Stock Trends*, by Robert D. Edwards and John Magee, first published in 1948. It is a difficult read, but remains the classic on technical analysis. 8th edition, St Lucie Press, 2001. The body of the book has not been changed, though new material has been added.
- *Technical Analysis Explained*, by Martin J. Pring, McGraw-Hill, 1991. This is an excellent book for those wanting a basic guide to using technical analysis. Studies on recurring events in economics and the stock market.
- *Forbes Guide to the Markets*, by Marc M. Groz, Wiley, 1999. This is an excellent "investing 101," both for the novice investor and for those investors who during the 1990s learned the technology of investing without understanding the principles behind the technology that enables people to make sound investment decisions.
- *The Intelligent Investor*, by Benjamin Graham, Harper Business. The classic on value investing. Written decades ago, but still in print. Graham was Warren Buffet's mentor.

Books on the History of Market Action

- *Rainbow's End, The Crash of 1929*, by Maury Klein, Oxford University Press, 2001. Tells the story of the events leading up to 1929 and its aftermath in a straightforward manner.
- *Modern Times*, by Paul Johnson, Harper Collins. Though not specifically about markets, includes economic history from the 1920s to the 1990s.
- *Extraordinary Popular Delusions & the Madness of Crowds*, by Charles Mackay, originally published in 1841, was reissued by Three Rivers Press in 1980.
- *Manias, Panics, and Crashes, A History of Financial Crises*, by Charles P. Kindleberger, Wiley, 4th edition, 2000.

The 1990s' Bubbles and Crises in the US and in Asia

- *Irrational Exuberance*, by Robert J. Shiller, Princeton University Press, 2000. An in-depth analysis of the US market in the 1990s to show why the bull market could not be sustained.
- *The Internet Bubble*, by Anthony B. Perkins and Michael C. Perkins, Harper Business, 1999. An insider's view into the world of Silicon Valley and why so many of the new high-tech companies were bound to collapse. Sobering reading.

- *The Downsizing of Asia*, by François Godement, Routledge, 1999. Most investors have little concept of how close Asia came to toppling the entire world economy during the 1990s. Indeed, if their crises had not occurred when prosperity was booming in the West, it is likely they would have caused a tidal wave across the world. If similar problems occur during the next few years while Western economies contract, it could indeed be wicked.
- *Japan, A Reinterpretation*, by Patrick Smith, Vintage Books, 1998. This book picks up the same theme as the one above, except it concentrates only on the problems in Japan. Is must reading to understand how potentially serious Japan's continuing economic problems are.
- *Asia in Crisis*, by Philippe F. Delhaise, Wiley, 1998. Another sobering account of the implosion of the banking and financial systems in Asia during the 1990s.

Cycles and Recurring Events

- *The Great Wave*, by David Hackett Fischer, Oxford University Press, 1996. As stated in our chapter on cycles (Chapter 10), I do not believe that events recur in a mathematically measurable way. David Fischer prefers to call them "waves" rather than "cycles," and has created a fascinating study of five great economic waves of history beginning in 1200. In 1996, he was already warning that we seemed to be coming to the end of a long-term up-wave.

The Psychology of Investment

- *Investment Psychology Explained*, by Martin Pring, Wiley, 1993.
- *The Crowd: A Study of the Popular Mind*, by Gustave LeBon, Cherokee, 1982.

Books about Holistic Economics

- *Friedrich Hayek, a Biography*, by Alan Ebenstein, St Martins Press, 2001.
- *The Wealth and Poverty of Nations*, by David S. Landes, W.W. Norton, 1998.
- *The Economics of Life*, by Gary S. Becker and Guity Nashat Becker, McGraw-Hill, 1997.
- *The Fourth Great Awakening & The Future of Egalitarianism*, by Robert W. Fogel, University of Chicago Press, 2000.
- *The Invisible Heart, An Economic Romance*, by Russell Roberts, The MIT Press, 2001.
- *The Road to Serfdom*, by F.A. Hayek.

SOFTWARE AND DATA VENDORS

There are dozens of information sources out there, and many of them offer
their services for free. But, be careful: you tend to get what you pay for. Among
my personal favorites are:

- *Data Broadcasting Corp. (DBC)* (800) 527-0722 x 719. DBC provides
  real-time market data to the individual investor. DBC transmits quotes on
  65,000 stocks, options, and commodities.
- *Dial/Data* (718) 522-6886. Since 1972 has offered daily and historical
  prices for all types of securities for US, Canada, Europe, and the Pacific
  Rim.
- *Omega Research* 800-422-8587. Software vendor of Supercharts.
- *Media General Financial Services*, PO Box 85333, Richmond, VA 23293,
  fax: (804) 649-6739, web site: www.mgfs.com They provide a range of
  data services. Their Constant Dollar Dow chart is reproduced on
  pp. 150–151 of this book.

MAGAZINES AND NEWSPAPERS

- *Wall Street Journal, Barron's*. Both offer mainly US financial and
  economic news and many of the statistics we talk about in this book.
  Available on most newsstands, and around the world in major cities.
- *The Economist*. A weekly magazine published in London, offering a global
  overview of world news from a European perspective. Even if you don't
  invest in Europe, the different perspective on US and world news is worth
  reading. Most local newsstands carry it in major cities. Access via net:
  www.economist.com
- *Financial Times*. A quality British daily financial newspaper that offers a
  European perspective on both US and world events with particular
  reference to how they affect markets. It publishes US and non-US market
  data on a daily basis. Major US and world newsstands usually carry it.
  You can access their web site at: www.ft.com
- *Investor's Business Daily* (a 5-star paper), PO Box 6114, Inglewood, CA
  90312-6114, phone: 800 831 2525. Packed full of market data, charts, and
  information on companies, as well as major news stories. In addition to its
  being a daily newspaper, the company also publishes stock charts. Sadly,
  it's not sold outside the US.

CHART SERVICES

- *Value Line Publishing*, 220 East 42nd Street, 6th Floor, New York, NY 10017, www.valueline.com Provides information and charts on stocks, both online and in paper form.
- *Securities Research Company*, phone: (877) 388-4502. Publishes Security Charts, both in book form and online.

Index

The International Harry Schultz Letter (also known as *Harry Schultz Life Strategies*) has been published continuously for 38 years. Each issue analyzes & forecasts trends of major global financial markets, gives specific advice, & brings you unique information of political, social and ideological trends, that affect both your investments & your entire lifestyle.

 Yes, please sign me up for **HSL!!**

1 year via airmail or e mail: $285

6 months via airmail or e mail: $159

Special Introductory offer: A three-month subscription for $99 of the *International Harry Schultz Letter* for readers of this book (coupon must be enclosed.) *HSL* is also available by fax. Ask for details.

Name: _____

Address: _____

City: _____ State & Zip code: _____

Phone # _____ Fax # _____

e mail address: _____

❑ MC ❑ Visa ❑ Check or International (Postal) Money

order enclosed

Card # _____

Expiration Date: _____ Visa only CVV2 code ___/___/___/___/

(Last 3 digits appearing in signature area on back of card.)

for the amount of US $ _____ Date: _____

Signature: _____

Mail to HSL, PO Box 622, CH-1001 Lausanne, Switzerland

or FAX (credit card payment only) to subscription office in Costa Rica:

Fax: 011 (506) 234 0433 (from USA/CDN).

Or Fax: 00 (506) 234 0433 (from elsewhere)

e-mail: HSLmentor@racsa.co.cr

For non subscription matters:

Harry Schultz's personal e mail: cameleon1@compuserve.com

fax: (377) 9770-3148 (that's in Monte Carlo)

"Gold Charts R Us"

It's *the world's only* gold chart service, with individual gold mine charts, bearing individual multiple buy/sell prices for each gold mine, plus multiple stops & targets, & it's weekly! It's unique & magical. Available by email & fax.

Harry Schultz, known as the gold guru in the roaring gold bull market of the late 1970s, is back at the head of the pack again with a service that was born just in time for the 2nd phase of the new gold bull market.

"Buy & Hold" doesn't work in the gold market. It doesn't really work in the general stock market anymore either, but in emotional golds, it never did, as golds are the most volatile of *any* stock group!

This is going to be a long bull market, lasting at least through 2004, with all the gyrations that go with an emotional market. It's a market with more opportunity than other markets as we can continue to sell, buy back, sell, thus compounding our profits. Those unenlightened fellow gold advocates who just buy & hold will not make more than modest gains & some will be scared out of positions during really sharp sell-offs. Remember, gold fell 50% during the middle of the last big gold bull market in the 70s. As bullion fell 50%, many individual shares fell 60–80%. Many gold holders sold, took losses in midst of a gold bull market. To prevent losses we use stops. U never know whether a pathway puddle of water is 12" deep or 1" deep. So watch where U walk! That's where *GCRU* guides you. Our handholding tells you when to take profits, when to buy more & again, precisely, not vague "buy TNX now" advice. We are precise, with loss aversion & profit maximization as our parameters.

☺ Stay in the sunshine of gold's glow.

– Your very own alchemist-guru, **Uncle-Harry**

"If it's Wednesday it's Gold Charts R Us."
The price is only US$100 a month, a sum easily absorbable from profits in trading. Useful advice doesn't cost; it pays. Subscriptions can be for 3, 6, 9 or 12 months. Quite frankly, we've been overwhelmed with the reception to *GCRU*. Lots of subscriptions & letters of thanks. It's an idea that met a sudden need as the gold market burst into bloom in early 2002. Email us at

HSLmentor@racsa.co.cr or fax Costa Rica 506-234.0433.
Or write: *HSL*, PO Box 622, CH-1001 Lausanne, Switzerland.

Want an (almost) *weekly stock market update*?

(with charts & data & VERY specific <u>stock recommendations</u>
both *long & short!* (with individual charts)

No one else does this. We don't know why they don't

We call it FMU: *Full Market Update*, a catch-all title

It's an auxiliary service to the *Int'l Harry Schultz Letter*.

Only HSL subscribers are eligible to subscribe to *FMU*. It's
dirt cheap but it's pay dirt!

It's only US$125 a year for aproximately 31 weekends a year
(in between *HSL* issues). It comes out on Mondays in time for
the NY opening.

It covers stocks, bonds, gold, & more.

Plus some pithy news as background.

When you subscribe to *HSL*, tell the reader service dept you
want *FMU* also. It's the cheapest $125 you ever spent in the
investment world.

Email us at HSLmentor@racsa.co.cr
or fax Costa Rica 506–234.0433.
or write: HSL, PO Box 622, CH-1001 Lausanne, Switzerland.

You'll be happy in the family of Uncle Harry

with the *Harry Schultz Letter* & *GoldCharts R Us* & *Full Market
Update*